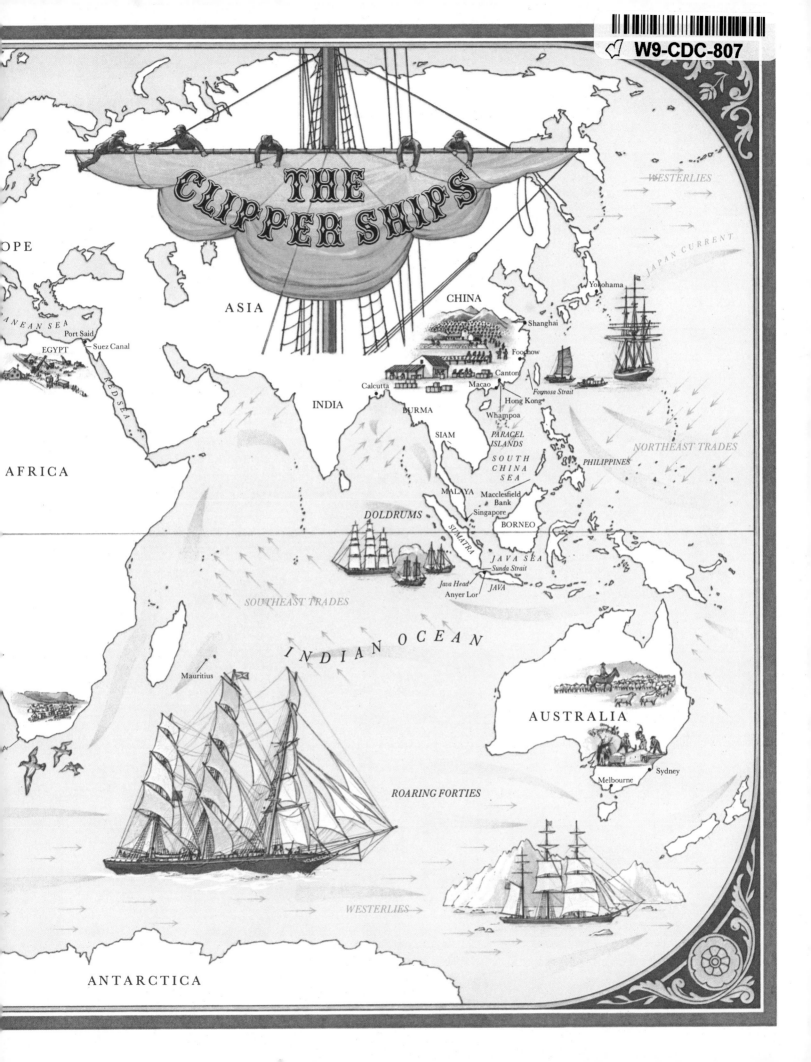

# THE CLIPPER SHIPS

*The Seafarers* THE CLIPPER SHIPS

*The Cover:* En route to San Francisco
during her maiden voyage, the clipper ship
*Golden State* slashes across a stretch of
the wintry Atlantic ahead of a rival clipper
in this painting by Leslie A. Wilcox.
The swift *Golden State* was launched in
New York in 1853 and sailed the great
trading routes of the world for 33 years.

*The Title Page:* Cast in 1869, this brass bell
—measuring 13 inches both in height
and in diameter—hung near the forecastle
of the *Cutty Sark,* the queen of British
clippers. The ship's lookout rang the bell
to announce the time, warn of fog and
tell when the crew was weighing anchor.

*The Seafarers*

# THE CLIPPER SHIPS

*by A. B. C. Whipple*

## AND THE EDITORS OF TIME-LIFE BOOKS

TIME-LIFE BOOKS, ALEXANDRIA, VIRGINIA

Time-Life Books Inc.
is a wholly owned subsidiary of

# TIME INCORPORATED

FOUNDER: Henry R. Luce 1898-1967

*Editor-in-Chief:* Henry Anatole Grunwald
*Chairman of the Board:* Andrew Heiskell
*President:* James R. Shepley
*Editorial Director:* Ralph Graves
*Vice Chairman:* Arthur Temple

## TIME-LIFE BOOKS INC.

MANAGING EDITOR: Jerry Korn
*Executive Editor:* David Maness
*Assistant Managing Editors:* Dale M. Brown (planning),
George Constable, George G. Daniels (acting),
Martin Mann, John Paul Porter
*Art Director:* Tom Suzuki
*Chief of Research:* David L. Harrison
*Director of Photography:* Robert G. Mason
*Senior Text Editor:* Diana Hirsh
*Assistant Art Director:* Arnold C. Holeywell
*Assistant Chief of Research:* Carolyn L. Sackett
*Assistant Director of Photography:* Dolores A. Littles

CHAIRMAN: Joan D. Manley
*President:* John D. McSweeney
*Executive Vice Presidents:* Carl G. Jaeger,
John Steven Maxwell, David J. Walsh
*Vice Presidents:* Nicholas Benton (public relations),
John L. Canova (sales), Nicholas J. C. Ingleton (Asia),
James L. Mercer (Europe/South Pacific), Herbert Sorkin
(production), Paul R. Stewart (promotion),
Peter G. Barnes
*Personnel Director:* Beatrice T. Dobie
*Consumer Affairs Director:* Carol Flaumenhaft
*Comptroller:* George Artandi

## The Seafarers

Editorial Staff for *The Clipper Ships:*
*Editor:* Jim Hicks
*Designer:* Herbert H. Quarmby
*Chief Researcher:* W. Mark Hamilton
*Picture Editor:* Peggy L. Sawyer
*Text Editors:* Anne Horan, Stuart Gannes, Gus Hedberg,
Sterling Seagrave
*Staff Writers:* Michael Blumenthal, Kathleen M. Burke,
Kumait N. Jawdat, Lydia Preston, Teresa Pruden,
David Thiemann
*Researchers:* Philip Brandt George, Sheila M. Green,
Ann Dusel Kuhns, Trudy W. Pearson, Jeremy Ross,
James R. Stengel
*Art Assistant:* Michelle René Clay
*Editorial Assistant:* Ellen P. Keir

Special Contributor
Barbara Hicks (Research)

Editorial Production
*Production Editor:* Douglas B. Graham
*Operations Manager:* Gennaro C. Esposito,
Gordon E. Buck (assistant)
*Assistant Production Editor:* Feliciano Madrid
*Quality Control:* Robert L. Young (director), James J. Cox
(assistant), Michael G. Wight (associate)
*Art Coordinator:* Anne B. Landry
*Copy Staff:* Susan B. Galloway (chief), Anne T. Connell,
Sheirazada Hann, Celia Beattie
*Picture Department:* Betsy Donahue,
Nancy Cromwell Scott

Correspondents: Elisabeth Kraemer (Bonn); Margot
Hapgood, Dorothy Bacon, Lesley Coleman (London);
Susan Jonas, Lucy T. Voulgaris (New York); Maria
Vincenza Aloisi, Josephine du Brusle (Paris); Ann
Natanson (Rome).
Valuable assistance was also provided by: Enid Farmer
(Boston); Diane Asselin (Los Angeles); John Dunn
(Melbourne); Carolyn T. Chubet, Miriam Hsia
(New York); Mimi Murphy (Rome); Janet Zich
(San Francisco); Peter Allen (Sydney); Nancy Friedman
(Washington, D.C.).

*The Author:*
A.B.C. Whipple, a former Assistant Managing Editor of Time-Life Books, is an avid sailor and student of maritime history. He has written 10 books about ships and the sea, including *The Whalers* and *Fighting Sail* in The Seafarers series and a general history, *Tall Ships and Great Captains.*

*The Consultants:*
John Horace Parry, Gardiner Professor of Oceanic History and Affairs at Harvard University, is a renowned maritime historian. After he received his Ph.D. at Cambridge University, he fought in World War II, rising to the rank of commander in the Royal Navy. He has published many historical studies such as *The Discovery of the Sea, Trade and Dominion* and *Europe and a Wider World.*

Philip Chadwick Foster Smith, the author of eight nautical books, is curator of the Philadelphia Maritime Museum. Previously, he was in charge of the maritime collection at the Peabody Museum in Salem, Massachusetts, and served as managing editor of *The American Neptune,* a journal devoted to nautical history.

William Avery Baker is curator of the Hart Nautical Museum at the Massachusetts Institute of Technology, where he earned his degree. A naval architect and engineer, he has drawn the reconstruction plans for 22 historic sailing vessels.

David R. MacGregor, who was educated at Cambridge University, is a noted author, draftsman and marine artist. His paintings have been exhibited in London, and his carefully researched ship plans are sold around the world. Among his books are *The Tea Clippers* and *Fast Sailing Ships.*

For information about any Time-Life book. please write:
Reader Information. Time-Life Books.
541 North Fairbanks Court. Chicago. Illinois 60611.

TIME-LIFE is a trademark of Time Incorporated U.S.A.

Library of Congress Cataloguing in Publication Data
Whipple. Addison Beecher Colvin. 1918-
  The clipper ships.
  (The Seafarers)
  Bibliography: p.
  Includes index.
  1. Clipper ships.   I. Time-Life Books.
II.   Title.   III. Series: Seafarers.
VM19.W54        387.2'2        79-24764
ISBN   0-8094-2679-X
ISBN   0-8094-2678-1 lib. bdg.

# Contents

# Ships to stir the seafaring heart

"She was a perfect beauty to every nautical man," one clipper captain said of his vessel. "She could do everything short of speaking." Never before had ships stirred seafarers quite the way clippers did. The pride—and hyperbole—of their masters knew no bounds. "Last trip I astonished the world," boasted one captain after a record-setting passage halfway around the world. "This trip I intend to astonish God Almighty."

American shipbuilders produced the first of these ships in the 1840s. The maritime culmination of a Yankee obsession with speed, they were the fastest, most beautiful wooden sailing vessels the world had ever seen—long and lean, with sharp bows, raked masts and a great cumulus of sail. Amazed by the clippers' performance, the British soon followed with versions of their own.

To see a clipper knife through wind-swept seas on a sprint from New York to San Francisco or between London and Hong Kong was to witness the quintessence of sailing. In winds that would cause others to reef sail, clipper captains flew every possible scrap of canvas, until the masts quivered at breaking point. Clippers rode tempests like sea birds, reaching speeds as high as 21 knots, making some 400 miles a day and setting records that would last forever.

Some of the finest portraits of clippers were created by marine artist J. E. Buttersworth, whose work appears on these pages. Buttersworth rendered each line with an affection rarely bestowed on inanimate objects—but that was only proper. Clippers, declared one admirer, seemed "to walk the water like a thing of life."

Bound for San Francisco, the newly launched Sovereign of the Seas hoists her royals in a fresh breeze off New York in 1852. Designed and built by the renowned Donald McKay, she sailed under the command of his brother on her maiden voyage, which took 103 days port to port. Her 258-foot hull displays the concave bow and the champagne-glass stern that were typical of clipper ships. She was acclaimed by The Boston Daily Atlas as "the longest, sharpest, most beautiful ship in the world."

While a storm jib gives the clipper Young America steerage way in a howling hurricane, her crew labors to haul in the main-topsail, which has flown loose from its spar. Built by the eminent New York shipwright William Webb in 1853, the Young America was a stout ship in bad weather, and once survived being knocked abeam by a whirlwind off Argentina. A favorite of shipping merchants because of her fast passages, she commanded top freight rates, often double what lesser ships earned.

Despite signs of ominous weather to starboard, the McKay clipper Westward Ho flies a full suit of sails, with triangular jibs at her bow, staysails between her masts, and starboard studding sails outrigged on her mainmast and foremast. Her mizzen course—the lowest square sail on her rearmost mast—remains furled only because it would be blocked on this heading by the huge spanker at her stern. The Westward Ho was so fast, said one sailor, that she ran "like a scared dog."

Preparing for a squall, the crew of the clipper Stag Hound takes in sail while another clipper, a schooner and a paddle-wheeler heel through the whiskery chop. The Stag Hound was one of the first of the sharp-bowed, long, "extreme" clippers, ranking as the largest vessel in the American merchant marine when she was launched in 1850. Built by Donald McKay in Boston, she inspired scores of imitators. "Every element in her," stated the Boston Atlas, "has been made subservient to speed."

With four masts, miles of rigging and an overall length of 335 feet, Donald McKay's Great Republic was the largest and most publicized wooden merchant sailing ship ever built in America. Lithograph publishers Currier & Ives commissioned this portrait from J. E. Buttersworth shortly after the vessel's launching in 1853—an event attended by 60,000 people. But just before the giant clipper set off on her maiden voyage, a fire in a bakery spread to her dock and burned her to the water line.

# Chapter 1

# The zenith of the age of sail

*Birthplace of the early clippers, New York City's waterfront wears a tranquil air in this 1853 lithograph. Brooklyn is seen beyond the East River.*

I n the 1840s a semaphore signal tower stood on Navesink Highlands, 250 feet above the treacherous spit of Sandy Hook, near the entrance to New York Harbor. The highlands commanded a sweep of open ocean bounded on the east by the Long Island shore and on the south by the New Jersey coast. From this height, incoming ships were visible more than 40 miles at sea on a clear day. On the crisp Sunday afternoon of March 25, 1849, a lookout was enjoying the panoramic view from his station under the tower's long, angular arms. The sea was speckled with whitecaps rippling toward the harbor before a fresh south-southeasterly. White sails flickered against the blue water as coastal schooners and brigs picked their way through the channels leading to New York's Upper Bay. Farther off, on the southeastern horizon, one sail in particular caught the eye of the lookout.

It was merely a white speck at first, but the lookout was riveted by the rate at which it grew: The ship was plainly traveling at great speed. Through his telescope he watched the speck resolve itself into a panoply of sails rising above the horizon, row by row. First, high atop the ship's three slender masts, her tiny skysails appeared; next came her royals; then, under those, her topgallants. Beneath the topgallants flew her wide, wind-taut topsails and mainsails. And puffing out sideways from the tips of her yards were tiers of studding sails.

Now the whole vessel was above the horizon, and there was no mistaking her type. The cloud on cloud of canvas she flung to the wind marked her as one of the awesome new China clipper ships. But, by the lookout's reckoning, none of these ships should be anywhere near New York Harbor this early in the spring. Months before, more than 40 vessels—only a handful of them clippers—had sailed from New York to China to pick up the tea crop, which in that region was usually ready for shipping in January at the earliest. So even the fastest of the returning ships should now be rounding the Cape of Good Hope or, at best, should be somewhere in the South Atlantic. Yet here, amazingly, was one of the clippers from the tea fleet.

On she came, racing before the wind, her acres of sails flashing in the afternoon sun. She looked for all the world like a ship in a painting, so slight was her vertical movement as she closed on Sandy Hook. An ordinary sailing ship would lift her bows and plunge with the seas. Not this one. As her sleek, jet-black hull sliced through the swells, the only visible motion was the white curl at her bow and an occasional toss of spray. She seemed to skim the surface of the water like a gigantic black and white bird—and abruptly she began to fold her wings.

With a flap and a flutter, her studding sails came in from her sides, making her look leaner and trimmer but scarcely reducing her speed. Then, a moment later, a blue and white square of bunting rippled to her masthead, the house flag of Howland & Aspinwall.

The lookout was already certain of her identity; through his glass he had just made out the golden Chinese-dragon figurehead beneath the vessel's bowsprit. Still baffled by her presence, he scrawled a message on his pad for the semaphore operator. The long arms atop the tower creaked out the message, visible across the bay to the telegraph operator

*The Sea Witch, described by The New York Herald as "the prettiest vessel we have ever seen," sails to her anchorage in Whampoa, downriver from Canton, in this Chinese painting. The swift tea clipper made a fortune for her owners and set at least a half-dozen records, some never broken, in her nine-year career.*

on Coney Island, who in turn tapped it out on the line to the Howland & Aspinwall offices in Manhattan. Though the clipper was still more than 20 miles from her berth at the foot of South Street, New York began to buzz with the news that the *Sea Witch* was home.

A pilot schooner came pitching out from the harbor, through the Narrows off Staten Island and past Sandy Hook, to greet the clipper. Up the rope ladder went the pilot who would guide the ship to her moorings. He was the first to congratulate Captain Robert H. Waterman on an astonishing feat: He had brought the *Sea Witch* to New York from Hong Kong, a voyage that only recently had taken up to six months, in 74 days.

This was not the first time that Waterman had broken the record for the run from China to New York. On the *Sea Witch's* second voyage two years earlier, Waterman had raced home from Canton in 77 days. In fact, before the *Sea Witch* had been built, he had brought the swift, rakish cotton freighter *Natchez*—a forebear of the clippers in some respects—from Portuguese Macao, off the China coast, to New York in 78 days. Each of these astounding runs had been hailed as unbeatable by the South Street merchants. Now Waterman had shattered his own best time by three whole days, and some of the old captains who joined the regular gathering at the Astor House bar the next morning asked one another if perhaps Captain Bob had not found some new route home.

He had not. Waterman had merely demonstrated that merchant sailing was well and truly in the throes of a revolution—and that no man could safely predict how fast these new ships could go. As it turned out, the achievements of vessels like the *Sea Witch* would never be equaled in the history of sail.

For all its glories, the clipper-ship era came and went with a rapidity reminiscent of the oceangoing greyhounds themselves. It started in America in the late 1840s and ended in England only a generation later. And it never would have occurred at all had it not been for a felicitous set of circumstances. A tiny group of designers conceived and perfected the new breed of swift, large ships at the very moment in history when world-wide trade called for just such vessels. And, as an elite group of bold, hard-driving captains arose to command the new clippers, they received invaluable guidance from an American geographer who, by

charting the winds and currents of the oceans, devised new sailing directions that cut days and weeks off long-distance voyages.

The term "clipper" was derived from the word "clip," meaning "pace," as in "to go at a good clip." Long and lean, with knifelike bows, the clipper carried loftier masts and wider sails than ever seen before. With pardonable hyperbole, ship designers and captains claimed that a clipper's soaring sails included moonrakers, cloud cleaners, skyscrapers, stargazers and, atop them all, an angel's footstool.

Builders and owners dreamed up a set of ship names that matched the clippers' speed and breathtaking beauty. Gone were such workaday appellations as *Essex*, *Ellen*, and *Three Brothers*. The proud new clippers were called *Lightning* and *Stag Hound*, *White Squall* and *Hurricane*, *Meteor* and *Flying Cloud*, *Queen of the Clippers* and *Sovereign of the Seas*. So exultant were some of the names that shipper George Francis

*Junks and sampans glide past the buildings and pennants of the Western trading establishments of Canton. Although business was conducted with bland cordiality, Western merchants had to leave their ships downriver, could not bring firearms or women into the city, and were always under surveillance.*

Train mockingly wrote home from Australia: "*The Wings of the Morning* came in day before yesterday but the *Utter-Most-Parts of the Sea* has not yet been heard from. *Snail, Tortoise* or *Drone* I would suggest for the next clipper. I am tired of these always-a-little-faster names."

The original clipper ships were built solely for the profitable New York-to-China tea trade. With American customers willing to pay a premium for the freshest tea, speed of delivery became a primary concern for merchants. At first, only a few of the most farsighted shipowners were willing to make the huge investments necessary to construct and operate the clippers. Then, just as these vessels proved profitable on the China run, gold rushes in California and Australia drove the demand for express freight sky-high. Scores of new clippers were hurried to completion and sent down the ways. They became longer, leaner and swifter than ever. In the past, few oceangoing vessels had sailed faster than an average of six knots over a sustained period, and sailors had regarded 150 nautical miles as an excellent day's run. But by the 1850s, powerful American clippers routinely made 250 miles a day for days at a stretch. And in 1854 the majestic *Champion of the Seas* blasted 465 nautical miles downwind in a single 24-hour period—an average of almost 20 knots—to set a record that would never be beaten by a sailing ship.

Inevitably the fever spread to England and a fleet of smart British

*The entire story of 19th Century tea production is compressed into this anonymous painting by a Chinese artist. Grown and picked in the hills (top), tea leaves were cured in open sheds (middle), packed in chests and bargained for by merchants (bottom left), then ferried by small boats to the foreigners' ships lying at anchor (far right).*

clippers materialized to defy the elements and to race one another in sail-ripping, spar-cracking, deck-drenching dashes, carrying the tea from China to London or bringing bales of wool from Australia.

Not only did the clippers race one another, they nobly flaunted their canvas in the face of a steadily mounting challenge from the plodding but economical steamship. The oceangoing steamer had in fact preceded the clipper by nearly three decades and in the 1840s was poised to eclipse all merchant sailing ships. But not until the 1880s did one of these steamers attain the speed of the fastest clipper. By that time, most of the great clippers had disappeared from the seas.

The beginnings of the American clipper ship predated the American nation itself. From the colonial period onward, speed was of major importance in American ships. Parliament in London passed harsh laws that restricted colonial trade, and that consequently made smuggling—which required fast ships—highly profitable. During the Revolutionary War the Americans were successful in few naval battles: All but a handful of the vessels in the Continental Navy were sunk or captured. But swift American privateers won glory and profits by harassing British shipping. Similar privateers and fast frigates outsailed the Royal Navy in the War of 1812.

Among the by-products of the second war with Great Britain were the rakish, two-masted Chesapeake Bay privateers. These trim, lively little brigs and schooners of the Chesapeake, modeled on the speedy French luggers and frigates that had helped the American cause during the Revolution, became known as Baltimore clippers. Although they were not called ships by the 19th Century seamen—only three-masted, square-rigged vessels qualified for that appellation—the Baltimore clippers were direct ancestors of the true clipper ships, if only because of the whim of a rich merchant.

In 1832 Isaac McKim, a Baltimore trader, commissioned a Chesapeake shipyard to build a three-masted, square-rigged ship that would be modeled on the lines of the local clippers, and yet would be capable of sailing to China. McKim's new ship was large and handsome, sleek in profile, with a low freeboard and a narrow, V-shaped hull. But at 143 feet in length and 494 tons burthen, she could carry only one half the load of conventional full-bodied ships of her size. This did not concern the wealthy McKim, who spared no expense in her building and fitting out. The vessel was constructed with frames of live oak, and her hull was sheathed with copper. Her deck was lavishly adorned with mahogany hatch coamings and brass capstan heads, and her bow was topped with the figurehead of a woman. To McKim's satisfaction, she proved to be a lithe and extremely fast sailer. He named the ship after his wife.

The *Ann McKim* has often been called the first clipper ship. She was not. Her bow was not so bluff as those of the other ships of the 1830s, but it was still round instead of sharp. Her beam was 27½ feet, wider than that of later clippers of her length. And her keel sloped downward, from 11 feet at the bow to 17 feet at the stern, whereas true clippers would be distinguished by flat keels from stem to stern.

Still, there was no doubt that she was something special. With her

*The 19th Century Chinese tea chest above—which, unlike most tea chests, is equipped with a brass hasp so that it can be padlocked—may have been used as a presentation box for an assortment of particularly expensive varieties.*

svelte lines, she sailed into the wind far better than did most full-bodied, square-rigged ships of her time. In her prime she was considered to be the fastest merchant vessel afloat. But, because of her expensive fittings and limited capacity, she was not copied by other shipbuilders, who regarded her as a rich man's indulgence, Mr. McKim's pet ship. When the old grain merchant died in 1837, the *Ann McKim* was sold to the New York firm of Howland & Aspinwall, which by then was looking for fast ships to add to its China fleet.

Enter John Willis Griffiths. Son of a shipwright, he had been employed at Virginia's Portsmouth Navy Yard before moving to New York to work for the esteemed shipbuilding company of Smith & Dimon. An open-faced, genial young man with a genius for mathematical insights into shipbuilding problems, Griffiths became fascinated by the physical laws that apply to how a ship proceeds through the water. In the Smith & Dimon offices, Griffiths investigated the studies of an Englishman, Colonel Mark Beaufoy, who had tested the resistance of different solid objects when they were towed in a water tank. Beaufoy had determined that increasing the length of an object "exceedingly diminishes the resistance with which it moves." And, without applying his theories directly to ship design, Beaufoy recommended that "the bottom of a floating solid should be made triangular," or V-shaped, along its whole length.

By 1840 Griffiths had devised his own testing tank to duplicate Beaufoy's experiments and to measure the resistance of various shapes. He quickly became convinced that many of the accepted principles of ship design were wrong.

"Cod's head and mackerel tail" was the popular description of the hull that had dominated merchant sail for two centuries. The round cod's-head bow smacked and battered the waves as the ship moved through the water, riding up and over each crest. The narrow stern of the hull left a clean wake with a minimum of visible turbulence. Griffiths recognized that this design made a safe ship, comparatively dry on deck because the seas were shouldered aside. Dependable it was, but fast it was not, no matter how large the ships or how great their sail area. There was a limit, Griffiths concluded, to what sails alone could accomplish, because of the resistance of the round-bowed hull.

At the drafting tables of Smith & Dimon, Griffiths began to work on the design for a swift new vessel. Studying the lines of the *Ann McKim*, he deduced that it was her lean hull and narrow bow that made her faster than most of her contemporaries. A vessel with an even-sharper bow should therefore be an even-faster ship. Griffiths also envisioned a long, gracefully tapered hull, with the greatest breadth farther aft than on any earlier ship. And he was convinced that his tank tests had told him something more—that the finlike mackerel tail of most ships was causing drag, an invisible form of suction under their sterns that held them back. Griffiths' ship would have a stern with a fuller shape, so that the water running past the long, thin hull would slide smoothly astern.

Published in an influential shipping journal, Griffiths' theories were at first violently scorned by many older designers and ship captains. A cardinal principle of ship design, Griffiths' critics all affirmed, was that the bow must surmount the waves as it moved forward. Allow it to dig

## An ugly war that led to the clipper era

"This war with China," protested the English educator Thomas Arnold, "seems so wicked as to be a national sin of the greatest possible magnitude." The Opium War of 1840-1842 was wicked indeed: By military force the British were trying to compel China to accept imports of an addictive and destructive drug. By one of history's ironies, that reprehensible campaign contributed mightily, if indirectly, to the advent of the glorious clipper era.

Britain's East India Company began shipping Indian opium into China in the 1780s. Six decades later, demand was so great that China's annual payments for what a Chinese leader called "this vile and poisonous substance" exceeded the country's profits from tea exports by three million dollars. The human costs of the trade were as grimly apparent as the economic costs. One British observer, visiting a smoking house, reported: "The couches are filled with occupants who lie with an idiot smile upon their countenances. A few days of this fearful luxury will impart a haggard look to the features; a few months will change the strong man into a skeleton."

In 1839 a high-ranking Chinese official, enraged by

too deeply, they said, and the ship would slide into a solid wall of water beneath the wave crests. Smart young John Griffiths had worked out some interesting concepts in the flat calm of his testing tank, they conceded, but if he ever saw a ship plow into the 50-footers off Cape Horn, he would forget about his sharp bow. It would cut through those combers, all right—bringing them down onto the deck and imperiling the ship.

But Griffiths was convinced that a ship of his new design would be seaworthy as well as fast, and he set out to get a commission. In February of 1841 he prevailed upon the American Institute, a headquarters of marine architecture in New York, to exhibit a small-scale model of the ship he had in mind. Griffiths had no immediate takers for his model but, unbeknownst to him, events were occurring on the other side of the world that would prompt a pair of enterprising merchants to take a chance on his design.

About a year after Griffiths' model went on display in New York, British troops won a bloody victory in Canton, China, ending the two-year Opium War. Before the War, foreigners could trade with China only at Canton, and there under tight restrictions. Now a peace treaty ceded Hong Kong to the British and opened up four ports—in addition to Canton—to traders from all Western nations: Amoy, Foochow, Ninghsien and Shanghai. As a result, New York shipbuilders were swamped with orders for new vessels capable of making the voyage down the Atlantic, around the Cape of Good Hope, across the Indian Ocean, up through the China Sea and back, a round-trip distance of some 30,000 miles.

Americans were becoming avid customers for Chinese goods—tea, silks, cinnamon, firecrackers and much more. The United States, now more than half a century old, had entered an age of prosperity, and there was money to be had for luxuries as well as necessities. In Boston, Philadelphia and New York, city dwellers were forming an acquaintance with the many different varieties of Chinese tea—Hyson and Bohea, Imperial and Gunpowder, Lumking and Mowfoong—and were also learning about their perishability; the most delicate teas became moldy in sea air. With the East Coast cognoscenti clamoring to pay large premiums for the freshest tea, merchants began paying more to shipping companies that could deliver it within a few months instead of half a year. Suddenly there was money to be made for each day saved in transportation. Moreover, there was the promise of fabulous profits to the owners of the first tea-laden China trader to reach New York with samples of the new year's crop.

Among the shrewdest shippers were the Messrs. Howland and Aspinwall of New York, who had been in the China trade more than a decade. By 1843 they were dispatching several ships to Canton every autumn to await the first tea pickings and rush home. With the profitable tea market growing by leaps and bounds, Howland and Aspinwall decided to add another ship to their China fleet. Dreaming of the killing they could make with a vessel that was both large and fast, they decided to build a ship based on Griffiths' proposals. They commissioned the new ship from Smith & Dimon. She would be called the *Rainbow*.

The *Rainbow's* ribs were hardly rising from her keel when word of her

Britain's refusal to curb the opium traffic, ordered all stocks destroyed. Imperial soldiers seized 20,000 chests of the drug from English merchants and cast their contents into the Pearl River at Canton. There followed two years of naval skirmishes, in which China's antiquated junks proved hopelessly outmatched by Britain's warships. Forced to sue for peace, China signed the humiliating Treaty of Nanking in 1842. In addition to mandating the resumption of opium imports, the agreement ceded Hong Kong to Britain and opened five other ports to foreign commerce.

France and the United States then insisted on similar trade concessions. The British kept control of the lucrative opium traffic (they stayed in the business until 1915), but there was money to be made from trading in other products. American ships were soon plying the China route in increasing numbers, bringing back tea and handcrafted goods. The perishability of tea inevitably led to a need for faster ships, and America's clipper builders answered the call.

*Inside a Chinese opium den the proprietor offers a pipe to an addict, while other users loll in dreamy lassitude.*

Shipwrights and laborers swarm over New York City's vast, timber-strewn Smith & Dimon shipyard in this 1833 painting. A few years later, designer John Griffiths would rise from their ranks to become a pioneer of clipper ships. For both his work at the drafting board and his writings—he was editor of the periodical American Ship—Griffiths was widely regarded as the era's greatest contributor to the science of shipbuilding.

radical design spread along the New York waterfront, and soon a steady stream of merchants, ship designers and captains were ambling down to the Smith & Dimon yard to have a look. The older salts could scarcely believe their eyes. The new ship was as massive as the biggest Atlantic packets. But her bow was as sharp as that of one of the pert little Baltimore clippers, nearly concave on each side, and her stern timbers were rounded like the apple-cheeked bow of a proper ship. The *Rainbow* must be turned the wrong way around, they muttered. Put her rudder at the other end, sail her backward and she might get somewhere. Otherwise she would drive into the first big ocean swell she met and plunge straight for the bottom. Even the vessel's rigging irked the oldtimers: The tall masts Griffiths had designed would go by the boards with the first puff of a gale. A death ship if there ever was one, the veterans predicted, and soon they were calling her "Aspinwall's folly."

So pervasive was the criticism that William E. Howland and William H. Aspinwall grew faint of heart. Aspinwall decided to consult outside experts, particularly on the subject of those soaring masts. He dispatched an agent to England to obtain a second opinion about Griffiths' proposed combination of slim hull and lofty spars. In the meantime, work on the *Rainbow* slowed and Griffiths' new wonder waited, in danger of being stillborn, in the Smith & Dimon yard. What Messrs. Howland and Aspinwall did not know was that the *Rainbow's* competition was already taking form.

While Griffiths had been drafting his intricate designs on paper, a burly, hawk-eyed, sideburned veteran of the quarter-deck had been whittling away at a block of white oak, shaping a model hull that represented his own ideas for a ship that would excel on the China passage. Relying less on equations and coefficients than on his own practical observations, Captain Nathaniel B. Palmer was reaching conclusions that were just as radical as Griffiths'.

Captain Nat, senior to Griffiths by 10 years, had long familiarity with the sea. His childhood playground was his father's shipyard in Stonington, Connecticut, and he grew up sailing catboats on Long Island Sound. He first went to sea at 14 aboard a blockade runner in the War of 1812, then shipped out at 19 on a Stonington sealer. In 1820, at the age of 21, Palmer commanded his own sloop, the *Hero*, on a sealing voyage that took him so far down the South Atlantic that he became one of the first persons in history to sight the mainland of Antarctica. Palmer went on to build a reputation as an effective master during the 1830s, when he skippered cotton packets between New York and New Orleans and general cargo packets between New York and Liverpool. In January 1843 Palmer got his first opportunity to sail on the lucrative China run; his vessel was the bluff-bowed packet ship *Paul Jones*. During her plodding passage he began to speculate on the design of a ship that could make the run much faster.

Palmer's instinctive idea for a new sailing ship bore a striking resemblance to Griffiths' design for the *Rainbow*, with one significant difference. Besides a sharp bow and narrow beam, Palmer's hand-carved hull had what he called a "flatter floor." The inspiration for this feature came from the cotton ships Palmer had skippered for years: They had flatter bottoms than most vessels—for two reasons that had nothing to do with a deliberate design for speed. First, the cotton carriers' shallow draft enabled them to slip over the great bar of sand and mud at the mouth of the Mississippi River leading to New Orleans—a barrier that would thwart any large, deep-keeled, V-bottomed vessel. Second, the flat bottoms of these vessels allowed more efficient packing of the rectangular cotton bales. According to ship-design tenets of Palmer's day, the cotton carriers should have sacrificed a certain amount of speed for these advantages—but they did not. In fact, they had set new speed records for the run from New Orleans to New York.

During Palmer's stint on the transatlantic run in the 1830s, he had persuaded shipowner Edward Knight Collins to commission a couple of flatter-bottomed ships for the Liverpool trade. Palmer was convinced that a ship so designed would be able to outrun the conventional full-bodied packet ships that had dominated the route for the past 20 years. Soon Collins' Dramatic Line ships were averaging faster passages than any of the competition's.

Their flat bottoms, in fact, may have had nothing to do with their speed. Hydrodynamicists never have been able to determine if a flat-bottomed hull outperforms a hull with a V-shaped bottom. The Dramatic Line ships may have been faster simply because they were longer; marine architects do know that increased length definitely does permit a greater maximum speed. But while other factors may have been responsible, flat bottoms appeared to make Collins' Atlantic vessels faster—and Nat Palmer's subsequent espousal of this feature for ships on the China run would win almost universal acceptance.

Aboard the *Paul Jones* on its 1843 voyage was one William H. Low, who had been in Canton representing the New York shipping firm of A. A. Low & Bro., in which he was a partner. As the *Paul Jones* slowly made her way halfway around the world, Palmer and Low had many long evenings together. Settling back in the stateroom's leather couch, they would light up their after-dinner Havanas and study the merits of Palmer's ship model.

William Low had as much foresight as Messrs. Howland and Aspinwall, plus the courage of his convictions. The *Paul Jones* had hardly tied up to her wharf on the East River when A. A. Low & Bro. commissioned the Brown & Bell yard—located at the foot of Stanton Street, less than a mile from where the unfinished *Rainbow* sat in her stocks—to lay the keel for a ship patterned on Palmer's whittled model. And while the *Rainbow's* construction continued to be held up by the trepidant firm of Howland & Aspinwall, the A. A. Low & Bro. ship was rushed to completion. She was launched Friday, May 3, 1844, and was named the *Houqua*, after a much-admired Chinese merchant of Canton who had died the previous year.

At the *Houqua's* launching, *The New York Herald* called the ship "as sharp as a cutter—as symmetrical as a yacht—as rakish in her rig as a pirate—and as neat in her deck and cabin arrangements as a lady's boudoir. Her figurehead is a bust of Houqua, and her bows are as sharp as a pair of Chinese shoes."

*The image of urbanity in this portrait, clipper captain Nathaniel B. Palmer was so rugged that he sometimes stayed on deck continuously for weeks in stormy weather, catching short naps in a topside armchair. He had canniness to match: In his periodic role as a clipper designer, he secured a share in the ships he built, and so became one of New York's leading merchants.*

Was the *Houqua* a clipper ship? Not quite. But she was a long, lean, lofty-sparred forerunner, perhaps a greater departure from all her predecessors than the true clippers would be from her. With Captain Palmer on her quarter-deck, the *Houqua* sailed for Canton on May 31, 1844. She reached her destination in 95 days, 16 fewer than Palmer had taken on the *Paul Jones* the previous year. Her 90-day voyage home beat the *Paul Jones's* time on the same run by 23 days.

Although neither Howland nor Aspinwall ever admitted it, the launching of the *Houqua* must have helped persuade them to give the final go-ahead to Smith & Dimon to complete the *Rainbow*. By the time Aspinwall's expert had returned from England with a suitcase full of rigging plans, the *Rainbow* was nearly finished, and Griffiths shoved the British blueprints into his drawer. The *Rainbow* was launched on February 22, 1845, nearly nine months after the *Houqua*. The *Rainbow*, too, was more an immediate progenitor than a true clipper—sharper, leaner and loftier than any other large ship, even the *Houqua*, but not so extreme as the vessels that were to follow. Under the command of veteran Captain John Land—in his fifties and known to his crew as "Old Man Land"—the *Rainbow* sailed for China with high expectations for a speedy voyage.

Only a few days out of New York she suffered a setback. Piling on the canvas, Old Man Land, who by one account never opened his mouth except to bellow orders, had sent her racing down the Atlantic. Then, at the height of a stiff gale, all three of her topgallant masts came crashing down with a sickening series of cracks and bangs. Chopping through the tangle of lines, Land and his crew fished the spars aboard and repaired the damage while the *Rainbow* limped along under jury rig.

The mishap foreshadowed many such accidents that would occur during the clipper-ship era: So finely tuned were the new vessels' spidery networks of shrouds and spars that many clippers lost their top-hampers during their first voyages, before their captains had an opportunity to judge the amount of canvas the ships were capable of carrying under various weather conditions.

On this occasion the performance of the *Rainbow* was diminished by another factor. Because of the delay in her construction, she had sailed in the wrong season, leaving New York in the dead of winter and reaching the China Sea at the time of the adverse monsoon. Forced to tack into the teeth of the season's prevailng northeast winds, Captain Land took 102 days to reach Hong Kong. By the time he began the return journey with a valuable cargo of pekoe tea, the monsoon had shifted and the *Rainbow* had to sail into southwest winds. Still, she made the trip in 102 days. On that run, Land reported, his ship had attained speeds of 14 knots. Moreover, the *Rainbow* had set a new record for the whole passage out and back. And in just one voyage she had earned profits equal to twice the cost of her construction.

On her second voyage, that same year, the *Rainbow* made Hong Kong in 99 days and raced for home two weeks later with another cargo of tea. Storming up the Atlantic, Captain Land raised Sandy Hook in only 84 days, before any other returning ship had brought New York the news of the *Rainbow's* safe arrival in China. "We met no ship that doesn't know the looks of her heels. The vessel will never be built that can beat her,'' Old Man Land crowed to anyone who would listen.

This boast would soon prove exceedingly hollow. Howland & Aspinwall had already committed itself to faster ships that would outclass even the *Rainbow*. In fact, hardly had Captain Land departed on his first voyage than the *Rainbow's* owners commissioned Smith & Dimon to lay the keel for a new racer to send to China. Howland & Aspinwall ordered the new ship shortly after the firm's most famous captain, Robert H. Waterman, had electrified South Street by romping home from Portuguese Macao in only 78 days. His ship was the 130-foot cotton packet *Natchez*, one of the original speedy flatbottoms whose performance had so intrigued Captain Nat Palmer. It was true that Captain Bob had drawn a charmed lot of winds from Aeolus' bag on that run. In fact, he had not needed to tack the *Natchez* once during the entire voyage. Under normal conditions a packet like the *Natchez* would have taken weeks longer to cover the distance. At the end of that voyage, Waterman received a hero's greeting from New Yorkers, who were captivated by the vision of China only 11 weeks distant. And if Waterman could make a record like that in the 14-year-old *Natchez*, Howland and Aspinwall wondered, what could he do in a sharp new ship?

*The name of the venerated Cantonese merchant Houqua (right) was given to a clipper-ship precursor (below) and also became a synonym for integrity. Poor at birth, Houqua managed to amass a fortune of $26 million through impeccably honest dealings with Western traders.*

*The merchant ship Houqua loses her mainmast and upper sections of her mizzenmast as she heels over in a raging storm. In a 20-year career, the Houqua made handsome profits for her owners, A. A. Low & Bro., but encountered more than her share of misfortune—including being struck by a meteor. She eventually vanished after leaving Yokohama in August 1864.*

Again they turned to designer Griffiths. This time, however, Griffiths worked with Captain Waterman, who devised the new ship's rig and sail plan. It was a perfect match—the brilliant engineer and the daring captain—and the melding of these two talents produced what can properly be called a true clipper ship.

The *Sea Witch* had a bow even sharper than that of the *Houqua* or the *Rainbow*. Her hull lines were as rangy as a pedigreed whippet's. At 170 feet 3 inches in length and 33 feet 11 inches in breadth, she was almost exactly five times longer than she was wide (the length-to-breadth ratio of most packets was about 4 to 1). Perhaps because of the *Houqua's* great success, Griffiths gave the *Sea Witch* a flatter floor than that of the *Rainbow*. Above the water line the new ship's bow flared outward in graceful concave curves. No full-bodied bulges marred her midship lines, and her sleek stern was capped with a short, overhanging transom. Painted black with a single gold stripe, she sported an aggressive Chinese dragon for her figurehead. The *Sea Witch* was launched on December 8, 1846. She was Griffiths' masterpiece.

Yet it was Captain Waterman's contribution that provided the power to drive the *Sea Witch's* hull. At Waterman's behest, Griffiths made the *Sea Witch* the loftiest ship afloat. Her mainmast soared more than 140 feet, as tall as a 14-story building. It carried the usual mainsail, topsail and topgallant, with a royal above them, and atop them all a cloud-scraping skysail. The foremast and mizzenmast also carried five tiers of sail each. In addition, the *Sea Witch* was equipped to carry studding sails—called stunsails by seamen—on extended yards that reached out on both sides of her normal rigging, even up to her royals. The gaps between her masts were filled with a number of triangular staysails, and the stays leading out to the tip of the ship's long bowsprit were hung with an assortment of jibs and flying jibs. Finally, large spanker sails could be hoisted up the mainmast and mizzenmast for sailing close to the wind. Waterman's rig called for more sails than were normally used by a 74-gun warship three times the *Sea Witch's* size.

The *Sea Witch*, like her predecessor the *Rainbow*, attracted many visitors while she rose in her stocks in Smith & Dimon's yard. Captain Nat Palmer walked around her and gave his opinion that she was "likely to prove very swift afloat," although, he cautioned, her intricate rig could be sailed only "at great expense, to say nothing of wear and tear." Whatever the expense, Howland and Aspinwall expected handsome returns. So lucrative had the China trade become that they sent the *Sea Witch* off to Canton in a northwest gale, in December 1846, knowing full well that she would have to beat against the winter monsoons to reach China and that she would arrive too late for the first tea pick of 1847.

No doubt Captain Bob Waterman had a part in this decision, so anxious would he have been to set sail. Throughout his career, Waterman was in a hurry. A New York native, born on March 4, 1808, he shipped out at the age of 12 as a cabin boy aboard a China trader. He went swiftly up the ladder of promotion on the rigorous transatlantic packets, where many of the clipper captains would get their training. By 1829, at 21 years of age, he had earned the prestigious rank of first mate on the famous packet *Britannia*. Aboard that ship Waterman gained a reputa-

# The bloodlines of an American thoroughbred

When the first clippers appeared in America in the 1840s, they so astonished the world that they were hailed as a new breed of vessel. In actuality, the hull designs of these ships had evolved from three earlier sorts of American craft, shown here in profile views adapted from marine architectural drawings called lines plans. The drawings portray a vessel from the side, bottom, bow and stern. Each view includes three sets of lines—two straight and one curved—that indicate regularly spaced sections of the hull in three dimensions and convey an accurate impression of shape, much as do topographical lines on a map.

Typical 18th Century American-built ships such as the *Codrington*, directly below, were modeled after British merchantmen of the period. Short, bluff-bowed craft with well-rounded cross sections, these vessels could easily poke in and out of small American harbors, delivering goods from England and taking on colonial cargoes.

The war that broke out between Britain and France in 1793 crossed the Atlantic in the form of harassment of American shipping, prompting United States builders to construct hundreds of sharp-bowed brigs and schooners ideal for privateering and blockade running. During the War of 1812, these vessels came to be called Baltimore clippers because so many were built in that city; at the bottom of this page they are typified by the *Lynx*.

With the coming of peace in 1815, transatlantic trade was resumed in earnest, and by the late 1820s New York and Boston shipping firms were energetically competing for business, promising fast and regular service. The ships born of this competition were the giant Atlantic packets such as the *New York (top right)*. While full-bodied amidships for efficient cargo stowage, the new packets were longer, slimmer and faster than older merchant ships.

The next generation is represented by the clipper *Sea Witch (bottom right)*, which was even longer than the packet ships. And, like the smaller Baltimore clippers, she boasted a sharp bow and a fine stern. But the *Sea Witch* was more than the sum of her evolutionary parts. She amounted to a quantum leap in ship design and became the prototype for a generation of clippers.

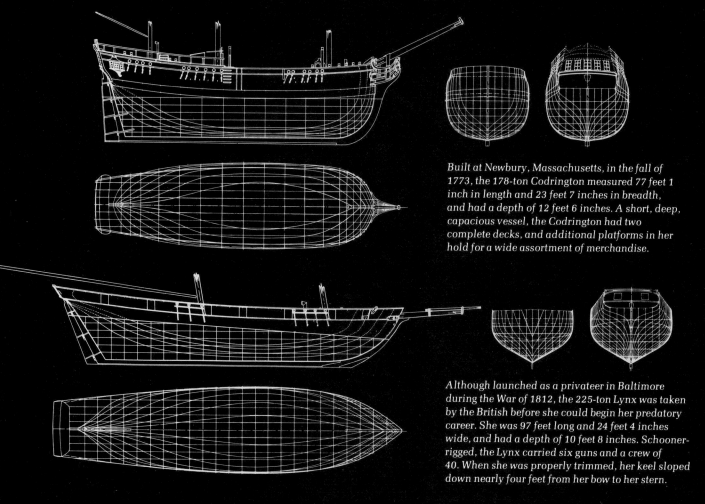

Built at Newbury, Massachusetts, in the fall of 1773, the 178-ton Codrington measured 77 feet 1 inch in length and 23 feet 7 inches in breadth, and had a depth of 12 feet 6 inches. A short, deep, capacious vessel, the Codrington had two complete decks, and additional platforms in her hold for a wide assortment of merchandise.

Although launched as a privateer in Baltimore during the War of 1812, the 225-ton Lynx was taken by the British before she could begin her predatory career. She was 97 feet long and 24 feet 4 inches wide, and had a depth of 10 feet 8 inches. Schooner-rigged, the Lynx carried six guns and a crew of 40. When she was properly trimmed, her keel sloped down nearly four feet from her bow to her stern.

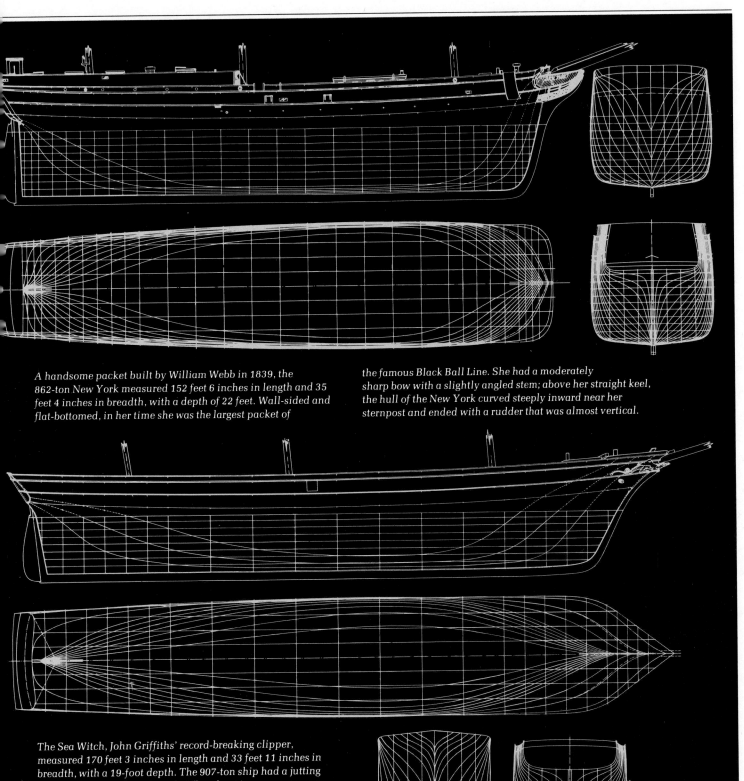

A handsome packet built by William Webb in 1839, the 862-ton *New York* measured 152 feet 6 inches in length and 35 feet 4 inches in breadth, with a depth of 22 feet. Wall-sided and flat-bottomed, in her time she was the largest packet of the famous Black Ball Line. She had a moderately sharp bow with a slightly angled stem; above her straight keel, the hull of the *New York* curved steeply inward near her sternpost and ended with a rudder that was almost vertical.

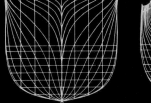
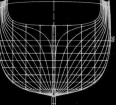

The *Sea Witch*, John Griffiths' record-breaking clipper, measured 170 feet 3 inches in length and 33 feet 11 inches in breadth, with a 19-foot depth. The 907-ton ship had a jutting stem and a razor-sharp bow that flared out in concave curves. Capable of packing 1,100 tons of cargo, the ship's hull was full-bodied amidships, with a rounded turn of the bilge. Aft of her mizzenmast, the clipper's hull was tapered with a graceful convex curve and ended with an angled sternpost.

tion as a tough and efficient officer—and a courageous one. The *Britannia's* Captain Charles Marshall later recalled how, in a North Atlantic gale, Waterman had dived overboard (presumably after fastening a life line to himself) to save a sailor who had fallen from aloft. Nor did it escape Captain Marshall's attention that the next day Waterman thrashed the same man for malingering. When Captain Marshall earned enough money to buy control of his own fleet of ships, one of his first moves was to promote Waterman to captain.

Waterman's first command was the packet *South America*, which he began driving back and forth across the Atlantic in 1833. His second ship was the *Natchez*, in which he made his record-breaking passage from Macao to New York. On that voyage Waterman had transformed the old cotton packet into a crack China racer. Using the ship's collection of spare spars for studding-sail poles, and throwing aloft every stitch of canvas he could dig out of the vessel's sail locker, Waterman had lighted a fire under the *Natchez'* tail, until she practically flew across the seas to her home port.

Now, aboard the *Sea Witch*, Waterman was determined to break the *Natchez'* record. The *Sea Witch*, with a hand-picked crew aboard, sailed from New York on December 23, 1846. Through the winter gales of the Atlantic and against the monsoon winds, Waterman pushed his new clipper hard, testing her ability to best the elements. Despite adverse weather during the whole passage, the *Sea Witch* reached China in 104 days, two days longer than the *Rainbow* took on her maiden voyage. Unlike the *Rainbow*, however, the new clipper came through with her top-hamper unscathed. And with favorable winds, she ran her cargo of tea back to New York in only 81 days. Less than two weeks later, Waterman and the *Sea Witch* were off again, this time for Hong Kong. The familiar struggle against the weather held her time to 105 days. Waterman raced the *Sea Witch* home in 77 days, breaking the record he had set in the *Natchez* five years earlier. But both of these creditable passages were about to be overshadowed by the *Sea Witch's* third voyage, the most remarkable China-to-New York run of the entire clipper-ship era.

To reach China on this trip, Waterman did not follow the usual route east around Africa's Cape of Good Hope and across the Indian Ocean. Instead, after raising anchor in New York Harbor on April 27, 1848, he took the *Sea Witch* west around Cape Horn at the foot of South America to deliver a cargo to Valparaiso, Chile, before crossing the Pacific for China. Altogether, the passage took 121 sailing days. Still, the *Sea Witch* was anchored in the harbor at Hong Kong that December, with several weeks to spare before the year's new tea pickings would be ready for shipment. In the first days of the new year, the clipper began to take on her cargo. At noon on January 9, 1849, the *Sea Witch's* hatches were sealed for the voyage, and Waterman bade Hong Kong good-by. At 7:30 that evening, with a fine breeze blowing out of the northeast, Captain Bob discharged the Chinese harbor pilot, and the *Sea Witch* set sail on a passage that would make history.

On this homeward trip Waterman would take the usual westerly course around Africa. Her sails straining above her long hull, her rigging thrumming and her masts groaning, the *Sea Witch* streaked across the

The house flags of shipping firms in New York—home port for most American clippers—are identified on this 19th Century broadside. The pennants of some firms—especially A. A. Low & Bro. (fourth row, fifth from left) and Howland & Aspinwall, whose name is spelled incorrectly here (fifth row, third from left)—were almost as well known in Hong Kong as they were in Brooklyn.

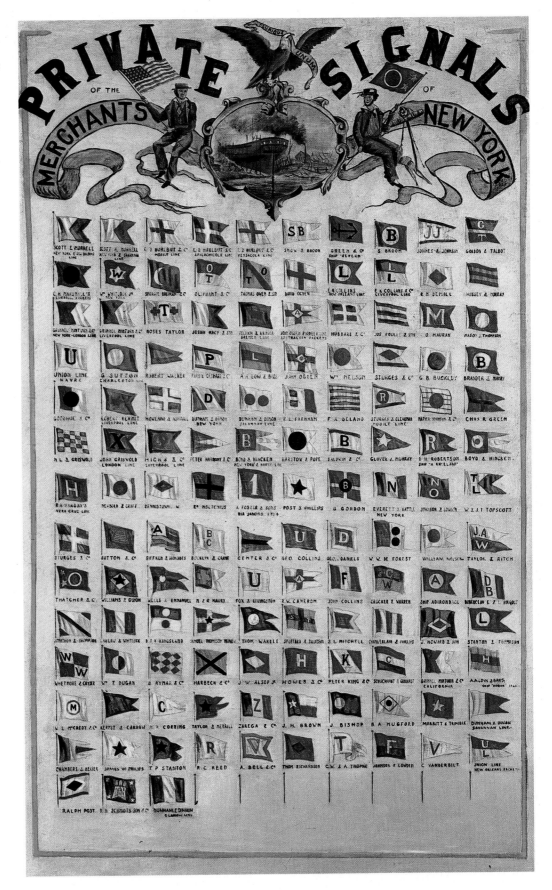

China Sea. The very first day she made 202 miles, traveling at a rate most sailing vessels could never hope to achieve. With Faustian confidence, Waterman ordered up the royals and studding sails. And, as if by agreement with the gods of the oceans, the *Sea Witch* began to race like a demon. Under a cloud of kites she logged 272 miles the second day, and on the third day she ran 262 miles.

This was Waterman at his best, keeping every shred of canvas on the *Sea Witch*, using the least slant of breeze and drift of current, clawing upwind through each gust. He had an intuitive feel for a ship under way, sensing when she was in perfect equilibrium with the wind and sea. He also had an almost eerie knack of guessing where the winds might be, and using them. For her part, the *Sea Witch* proved she could maintain her steady ocean-eating pace in almost any weather. On January 16, eight days out, First Mate George Fraser, who kept the *Sea Witch's* log, observed, "Light baffling airs through the day." Still, Fraser reported, the clipper eked out 65 miles.

Delicately picking his way through the myriad uncharted reefs of the China Sea, constantly on the lookout for Chinese and Malay pirates, Waterman made it to the Sunda Strait—the passage between the islands of Sumatra and Java—in only nine days. On January 17, as the *Sea Witch* slipped into the narrow strait, Malayan sampans shot out from the shore. Approaching the American ship, pidgin-speaking Malays offered coconuts and yams, ducks and chickens, mats and shells, monkeys and caged sparrows to the clipper men. As a precaution, Waterman armed himself and his officers, and ordered a close watch on the visitors. The Sunda Strait was notorious for foul play.

The *Sea Witch* was in luck—no pirates. She worked her way carefully through the reef-strewn waters, coming so close to the shore at times that the men could hear the parrots squawking in the jungle. On the night of January 17, a series of gusty squalls swept through the passage. Waterman anchored in the lee of an island. By dawn, Fraser noted, "the weather looking better," the anchor came up again. The *Sea Witch* skirted a rocky outcropping at the end of the strait, known to sailors as "Thwart-the-Way Island," and emerged into the dark-blue waters of the Indian Ocean. The looming heights of Java Head, redolent of sandalwood, receded astern. A fresh breeze sprang up, and Waterman set all sail.

The *Sea Witch* was scarcely out on the Indian Ocean when the wind died again. Still Waterman kept her moving through calms and light airs for a fitful week. Finally, on January 25, a succession of sharp rain squalls promised better weather, and the next day Fraser could record "strong breezes." The *Sea Witch* put her shoulder down and surged ahead. Now she began to fly. That day she ran 276 miles. On January 27 she made 292 miles, the next day 281 miles and the next, 282 miles. In his entry for February 1, Fraser wrote "strong trades" with a bold flourish of his pen, before recording a day's passage of 300 miles.

Within a fortnight the appearance of albatrosses and Cape pigeons announced the foot of the African continent. And at 3 a.m. on February 16, Fraser noted, "Cape Good Hope bore north true," as Waterman cut the corner. With the west coast of Africa just over the horizon, the *Sea Witch* picked up the southeast trades and went rushing northward. That

# An exotic trade's exquisite prizes

When America's venturesome clipper captains returned from a voyage to China, tea drinkers across the country rushed to pay top prices for the delicately flavored new pickings. But the clippers also brought a trove of less ephemeral temptations: Tucked among the tea chests were handcrafted Oriental wares coveted by almost every householder of the day.

The ravenous hunger for chinoiserie could be traced to the year 1785, when a pioneer of America's commerce with China, the *Empress of China*, arrived in New York with her hold weighted with porcelain as ballast. That casual cargo was immediately snapped up by the American public, and by the mid-19th Century Chinese artisans were supplying the United States market with a veritable cornucopia of merchandise—silks, porcelains, paintings, fans, silver dishes, ornate ivory *objets d'art*, and furnishings of polished wood and lacquer ware.

Westerners were particularly intrigued by the ivory carvers' skill. "Their mode of working is as much a secret as it was five centuries ago," reported an American merchant in 1844. "Many imagine the carvers have some method of softening the ivory, but I do not believe that. The art handed down from father to son has become perfect." The Chinese silversmith's workmanship was equally renowned. "He can manufacture any article in the most elegant manner or produce a pattern of forks at very short notice," observed one American. "The silver is remarkably fine and the cost of working it a mere song."

So brisk was the trade that by 1850, in Salem, Massachusetts, as much as one fifth of every household's goods was imported from China. Ladies' fans, a significant item in the trade, were brought in by the tens of thousands.

During the 1860s, as European factories began manufacturing inexpensive porcelains and Chinese craftsmen started producing cheap, gaudy items under the pressure of Western market demand, the traffic in finer goods tapered off. But by that time, China's largely anonymous artisans, with their command of vibrant color and intricate patterning, had left an enduring impression on a culture they would never see.

*A paper fan opens to reveal a watercolor vista of the Whampoa Reach anchorage near Canton, where American ships took on such wares.*

CARDCASE

FLOWER HOLDER

SOUP TUREEN

Three elaborately decorated containers
bespeak the mastery of China's
silversmiths. Westerners were astonished
by the low prices as well as the
beauty of these objects. "It is much
cheaper," said an American merchant, "to
have a splendid service of plate
in China than in any other country."

FLOWER BOAT

Ivory objects such as these, carved from elephant tusks that were imported to China from southern Africa, Siam and Burma, were among the most highly prized items of the China trade. Often set in finely worked wooden bases, these feats of craftsmanship inspired one American merchant to assert that "there are no such carvers in the world as the Chinese."

VASE

DECORATED ELEPHANT TUSK

Gleaming with a gilded view of the harbor at Macao, this handsome worktable with ivory fittings is one of thousands of lacquered furnishings exported to the United States during the 19th Century. The gilding was brushed on to a surface etched beforehand with a steel point.

SEWING TABLE

day she made the best run of her entire voyage, an amazing 308 miles. But in less than 48 hours the winds softened again. Waterman pushed on: 73 miles through light airs and overcast skies on February 19, then 158, then 128, 174, 198 and 183. Steadily the *Sea Witch* ran up the South Atlantic, moving surely but all too slowly for Waterman, who realized by this time that he stood a good chance of breaking his own record for the passage from China.

On March 5, Fraser wrote, "Rather more wind today," as the *Sea Witch* covered 220 miles. Then the wind fell off again, but Waterman still scratched out another 183 miles. On March 7 the *Sea Witch* crossed the Equator. A squally night on March 9 brought her into the latitude of the northeast trades. And the next day the clipper was roaring along, everything flying and bound for home.

By March 12 the whole crew talked about New York while they painted the ship so she would make a proper entrance into the harbor. Then, on March 20, a fierce squall struck out of the north-northwest, heeling the *Sea Witch* over hard and, wrote Fraser, "plunging bowsprit under." But the same sharp shape that made the clipper's bow likely to dip beneath the waves in these conditions also gave the *Sea Witch* "weatherliness," an ability to sail closer to the wind than her bluff-bowed predecessors. Waterman kept his course under double-reefed sails. The next day, near Bermuda, the *Sea Witch* was lashed by another storm, this time a northeaster, and Waterman reluctantly ordered triple reefs—and ordered them shaken out the minute the storm had swept past. Plunging through a "horrid head sea" in the wake of the storm, the *Sea Witch* entered the Gulf Stream. Finally the winds moderated; Waterman "set all stun-sails." And on March 25 he brought the *Sea Witch* up to her landfall under the gaze of the lookout at the Sandy Hook semaphore tower, completing the passage from Hong Kong in 74 days 14 hours actual sailing time—a record that was never broken.

The combination of John Griffiths and Robert Waterman was a natural alliance of designer and skipper, remarkable less in the fact of partnership than in the gifts of the partners. A third contribution to the success of the clipper ship was positively providential. While Griffiths and Waterman were launching the clipper era—with an assist from Nat Palmer —the man who set its course was at work in a stuffy office in Washington, D.C. Matthew Fontaine Maury had come to the aid of the clipper by a most unlikely circumstance. A farm boy from Tennessee who had left home to join the United States Navy, he had sailed around the world as a midshipman and risen to the rank of lieutenant when, after a visit home, he had been thrown from the top of a stagecoach. His broken leg had never properly healed, and for the rest of his life he walked with a limp.

The Navy, considering Maury unfit for further sea duty, assigned him in 1842 to its Depot of Charts and Instruments in Washington. In the depot's vault, Lieutenant Maury discovered a collection of thousands of ships' logs, including nearly every one that had been kept since the birth of the United States Navy. The logs had been relegated to the Depot of Charts and Instruments for want of a better place to put them. Dead storage to the Navy, they represented a treasury of information to Maury, for they held records of weather and sea conditions for every month of the year in all parts of the world. Once refined, this knowledge would constitute an aid to navigation as valuable as any instrument on the chart table or any volume in the bookshelf of a captain's cabin.

The lieutenant and his small staff immediately began organizing and compiling the hundreds of thousands of observations recorded in the logs. Maury also persuaded the Navy to enhance the collection by issuing to all its ships a standardized form requesting specific observations of weather, winds, currents and other hydrological and meteorological information. From the combined observations of the old logs and the new forms, he set about compiling a set of navigational charts to map the highways of the sea as they had never been mapped before.

His first area of concentration was the much-traveled passage from northeast America down the Atlantic to Rio de Janeiro. Here Maury made the first of many discoveries that would alter the traditional patterns of navigation and vastly reduce the time it took for a sailing ship to go from one port to another.

To most mariners in the 1840s, the chief obstacle in the run down to Rio was the great bulge of the South American continent at Cape São Roque, reaching out into the Atlantic nearly to the longitude of the British Isles. A skipper normally set a course out across the Atlantic, "running down his easting," as he called it, so as to weather Cape São Roque before turning south for Rio. But Maury, studying the countless observations in the Navy's logs, found that this was the wrong way to Rio, for two important reasons.

One reason was already known by most skippers, but they were unable to figure out what to do about it. The northeasterly trade winds of the North Atlantic and the southeasterly trades below the Equator were separated by bands of calm weather—the so-called doldrums. Most navigators resigned themselves to drifting through the doldrums, moving at a snail's pace for days and sometimes for weeks, until they had gone far enough south to pick up the South Atlantic trade winds. What Maury discovered from his study of the logs was that these bands of calm varied greatly in width: They were much narrower in some parts of the Atlantic than in others. Moreover, the width of the bands could also change according to the season of the year. "The calm belts of the sea," he wrote, "like mountains on the land, stand mightily in the way of the voyager, but, like the mountains on the land, they have their passes and their gaps." Maury thereupon charted the shortest passes through the equatorial doldrums of the Atlantic.

This contribution to navigation was doubly important because of yet another of Maury's discoveries. Mariners' tradition—and some guides to navigation—had it that, because of the prevailing winds off Cape São Roque, a strong current set in toward the land. Once a ship was trapped inside this current, warned the guides, it could lose days before it was able to work its way out.

The case was quite the contrary, as Maury discovered in the logs of the few skippers who had gone in close to Cape São Roque: Most had found no adverse current at all. Indeed, he wrote, "a few of them report the

For the decades he spent mapping global winds and currents on the basis of thousands of ships' logs, Matthew Fontaine Maury received honors from almost 50 learned societies, medals from European royalty, and the gratitude of clipper captains. But despite all his labors, Maury never rose above the rank of lieutenant in the United States Navy.

current in their favor." Maury also discovered that there was a narrow band of westerly winds near the coast. The favorable current and winds could actually help the captain make better time, so long as he held his ship close to the hitherto dreaded cape. This, Maury declared, was the "fair way to Rio."

In 1847 Maury published his discoveries in a volume titled *Wind and Current Charts*. On printed charts of the Atlantic, Maury superimposed a sprinkling of symbols that indicated the probable winds that a ship was likely to encounter. Accompanying this graphic correlation of his observations were recommendations on how to use those winds to the best advantage.

Veteran merchant skippers did not at first take kindly to such brash advice from a landbound naval officer who had seen less than a decade of sea duty. Then, in 1848, a merchant captain by the name of Jackson put Maury's charts to the test. Sailing out of Baltimore in the bark *W.H.D.C. Wright*, Captain Jackson ran from the Virginia capes to Rio in 38 days; the normal time was 55 days. Following the same charts, Jackson came home in 37 days. He had made the round trip in 35 fewer days than he usually required. The news took even less time to spread through the counting rooms of Baltimore, New York and Boston, aided by an editorial in the Baltimore *American*. Overnight, every shipowner and skipper wanted to get his hands on those newfangled charts.

Maury was ready for them with an offer that was so attractive they could hardly refuse it. He had prepared a 10-page *Abstract Log for the Use of American Navigators*; it distilled the information of his *Wind and Current Charts*, and accompanying it were 12 blank pages for the navigator to fill in during his next voyage. On receipt of this information, Maury would forward to the captain the latest, updated *Wind and Current Charts* free of charge.

By July 1848, only four months after Captain Jackson's voyage to Rio, Maury had received the abstract logs of four more ships on that run; they had saved an average of 10 days. By the end of the summer the reports were flowing in, and Maury and his assistants were busy trying to keep up with them.

Eventually Maury issued charts for all the world's oceans. These were supplemented by general sailing directions for the major trade routes. Later series offered more specialized information on the trade winds, monsoons, water-surface temperatures, storms, currents and even the distribution of whales.

The charts were steadily revised and improved as new reports poured in. By the end of 1851, Maury had heard from more than 1,000 captains. By 1854 he had about one million observations on the prevailing directions and velocities of the oceans' winds. He had received 380,284 observations on the Atlantic Gulf Stream alone. After collating all this new material, Maury expanded his charts by publishing what he called *Explanations and Sailing Directions*, which highlighted his discoveries and offered more general advice for long ocean passages.

By 1854 Maury had completed a definitive work that he titled *The Physical Geography of the Sea*. Combined with his earlier *Wind and Current Charts* and his *Sailing Directions*, Maury's *Geography* became

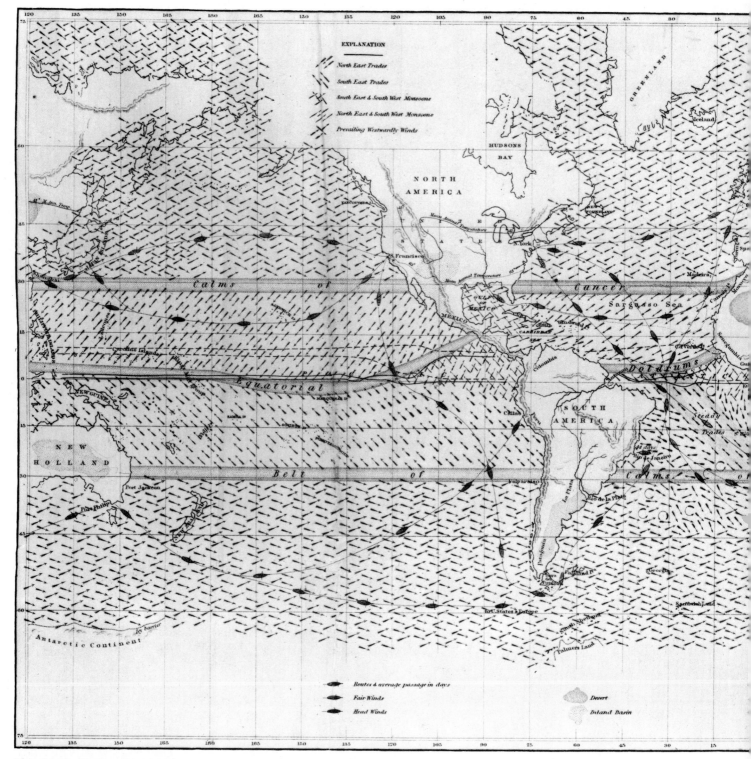

*This chart by Matthew Fontaine Maury indicates the directions of prevailing winds throughout the world. Long-distance routes that would best exploit the weather patterns are traced on the chart by series of schematic ships—the last one on each passage bearing a notation of the average time of the voyage.*

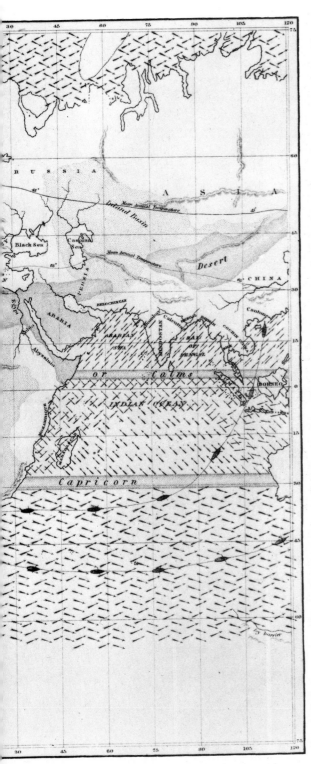

the essential guidebook for the mid-19th Century navigator. Besides guiding his "noble-hearted mariners," as he called his correspondents, on the fair way to various ports, Maury offered such intriguing and useful general information as:

☐ The Mozambique Current, flowing southeastward in the South Pacific and Indian Oceans, is 1,600 miles wide, nearly as broad as the entire length of the Atlantic Gulf Stream.

☐ The tides in the Atlantic are higher than those in the Pacific, with consequent differences in tidal-current velocity in some regions.

☐ The Atlantic is the stormiest sea in the world; the Pacific—true to its name—the most tranquil.

☐ Winds have little influence upon the major currents of the sea. The Gulf Stream, for example, runs much of its course right in the "wind's eye." So does the Japan Current in the Pacific.

☐ The Gulf Stream is "roof-shaped," i.e., slightly higher in the middle, with its surface waters flowing off to either side. The "runoff," as Maury called the flow, is too shallow to affect the deep hull of a ship. But the navigator is able to determine whether he is south or north of the stream's center by lowering a boat on a line; it will drift off to one side or the other with the flow.

☐ The southeast trade winds are stronger than the northeast trades because they predominate in the Southern Hemisphere, which is cooler than the Northern Hemisphere. Similarly, all trade winds are stronger during their hemispheric winter than in summer.

Maury's charts and *Sailing Directions* cut days and weeks off a vessel's passage. American ships, with their navigators using Maury's charts, began to circle the globe in a third less time than before. By 1851 the average merchant ship's time around the Horn to California was pared by more than 40 days, and clipper captains did even better. Some captains wrote Maury that, by avoiding the storm areas indicated on his charts, they had completed their voyages without reefing topsails more than once or twice.

Already many navigators were referring to Maury as the "Pathfinder of the Seas." Captain Phinney of the clipper *Gertrude*, sending in his contribution to what he called Maury's "great and glorious task," acknowledged that "until I took up your work I had been traversing the ocean blindfolded."

So, in a sense, the American clipper-ship era was designed by men like John Griffiths and Nat Palmer, ushered on stage by captains like Robert Waterman, and guided to greatness by Matthew Fontaine Maury. But it received its most powerful impetus from a man who had never seen a clipper. In January 1848 a carpenter named James Marshall, cleaning out a sluice at Sutter's Mill in California, noticed some nuggets glittering in the sand. He picked them up to examine them, and then beat one of them between two stones. The nugget did not shatter, as iron pyrites—fool's gold—would have, but obligingly changed shape when pounded. Marshall's pulse quickened, and so did that of the whole nation when news of his discovery got out. In California, a remote territory that could be reached from the populous Eastern United States only by a long trek or a longer voyage, James Marshall had found gold.

# Chapter 2

# A golden lure for clipper builders

The ribs of a new ship rise above a jumble of timber at Donald McKay's East Boston shipyard, where 32 clippers were built between 1850 and 1869.

**D**uring the spring of 1849, one of the strangest mooring procedures in the history of seafaring became a customary occurrence in the inner harbor of San Francisco Bay. It was a sight that would have astounded even the saltiest dock hand in any saner port. First, a ship would appear at the Golden Gate, the narrow entrance to the bay; usually it would be a bark or packet from New York or Boston, weatherworn and bedraggled from her arduous journey around Cape Horn, but normal enough in her actions as she approached. Gliding past the little island of Alcatraz and hooking around to the west, the vessel would steer directly for the crowded anchorage off North Beach at the foot of Telegraph Hill.

At this point the ship's behavior became decidedly bizarre. Ordinarily a captain would bring his ship into an anchorage under reduced sail, let go anchor and send the crew aloft to furl the sails neatly on their yards before the passengers, if any, were rowed ashore. But, as likely as not, a ship fetching up in San Francisco in 1849 would bear down on the harbor under full sail, drop anchor, let go her braces and sheets, and immediately begin debouching passengers over her gunwales as if she were expected to explode at any moment.

And an odd lot of passengers they were. Some carried paper parasols as if they were going to the Sudan, while others were bundled in furs and arctic gear. Many struggled to off-load a variety of exotic equipment, ranging from oddly shaped picks and shovels to cumbersome machines that might have been lifted from a patent officer's nightmare. Still others, unable to find a boat, dived into the bay to swim ashore. Frequently the ship's crew joined in the stampede, and in the space of a few minutes the captain was standing on the quarter-deck of an otherwise abandoned ship, her sails fluttering loosely in the breeze and only the harbor pilot left aboard to console him.

For all their comic-opera quality, such scenes were entirely natural at that time and in that place. This was gold-rush San Francisco, the seaside recipient of a motley army of fortune seekers who knew almost nothing of the California wilderness and still less of the techniques of extracting gold from the earth, but who were propelled by one thrilling conviction—that they were going to get very, very rich.

Although the first reports of a gold strike in the foothills of the Sierra Nevada had been greeted with healthy skepticism in the East, the evidence soon became undeniable. In December 1848 President James Polk had officially recognized the magnitude of the discovery by announcing that "the accounts of the abundance of gold in that territory are of such an extraordinary character as would scarcely command belief were they not corroborated by authentic reports." At about that same time, a small chest containing some $3,000 worth of nuggets and flakes from the California gold fields was put on view at the War Office in Washington. Each day a crowd gathered before the display, mesmerized by its promise of easy wealth. Meanwhile, an excitement verging on delirium spread throughout the country. From the hardscrabble farms of New England to the coal mines of Pennsylvania, a vast legion of men resolved to head at once for the far side of the continent to share in the harvest of riches.

THE WAY THEY GO TO CALIFORNIA.

Forty-niners use every conveyance possible—and some that are not—as they set out for California in this contemporary cartoon of the gold rush. Clipper ships, although they gave passage to many would-be prospectors, actually did a greater business in freight, hauling eagerly awaited supplies to the West Coast at a time when no large-scale overland transport existed.

Virtually every vessel on the East Coast that showed the slightest sea-going capability was pressed into service to tote the adventurers. In the period from April 1847 to April 1848, a total of only 13 vessels from Atlantic ports had called at San Francisco—then a slumbrous town with barely a thousand inhabitants; in 1849 no fewer than 775 vessels from the East Coast reached the new Golconda. Only a dozen or so clippers were then in existence, and most of these were busy running between China and New York. The sole clipper to join the 1849 rush was the *Memnon*, which easily set the record for the passage from New York, arriving in San Francisco on August 28, 1849, after 122 days at sea. Prior to this sprint, 200 days was considered a respectable time for the 15,000-mile voyage around Cape Horn.

Merchants back East quickly realized that there was a great deal of money to be made by shipping freight as well as people to California. The population of San Francisco was growing at a phenomenal rate—it would pass the 20,000 mark by the end of the year—and prices were out of control. A five-dollar barrel of flour sold for $50. A four-month-old penny newspaper from back East sold for one dollar; so did one egg. A pack of cards cost five dollars. Clearly, a ship that could make three voyages while the competition made two would be a money spinner.

*Combining a dreamer's vision with an engineer's practicality, Donald McKay designed 12 of the 13 clippers that achieved runs of 400 miles or more in one day. Yet he was never complacent: "I saw something in each ship which I desired to improve upon," he said.*

As soon as they could manage it, other clipper owners diverted their vessels from the China trade and sent them racing around the Horn. All of them were out to better the *Memnon's* time. On May 6, 1850, the A. A. Low & Bro. clipper ship *Samuel Russell* arrived in San Francisco 109 days after leaving New York. She was loaded to her scuppers with 1,200 tons of merchandise and flour that earned a stupendous profit. Two and a half months later, the *Sea Witch*, now skippered by Captain Robert Waterman's former first mate, George Fraser, came surging up to the Golden Gate in the amazing time of 97 days from New York, despite having encountered violent storms off Cape Horn. Her cargo, which cost $84,626 in New York, was worth $275,000 in San Francisco, nearly four times the clipper's construction cost.

News of these passages had a predictable effect. In the autumn of 1850 the shipyards of New York and New England, already busy building clippers for the China trade, fairly exploded with this new impetus. A long row of clipper-ship skeletons rose on the shores of New York's East River, where as many as 10,000 men worked in the yards from dawn to dusk. The sounds of sawing and hammering echoed across the river, and the air for blocks around was filled with the smells of wood shavings and pitch. The clipper-ship era was under way in earnest.

During the next 10 years, hundreds of clippers—most of them following Matthew Fontaine Maury's recommended route—would run their easting down to Cape São Roque, turn southwestward and thrash through the Cape Horn gales in sail-thundering voyages such as had never been imagined before. This passage called for a new type of clipper ship, larger than the China clippers so that they could carry more merchandise, and stouter so that they could withstand the violent weather off Cape Horn.

To the public at large, the clippers built for the California run were the stuff of legend—partly because they accepted the worst punishment nature could throw at them and almost insolently turned it into speed; partly because they were associated with the greatest adventure the new nation had ever known; and also, more fundamentally, because they represented an astonishing achievement of the shipbuilder's art. The demands of their design were such that the men who constructed these vessels won the status of popular heroes. And one member of their ranks—Donald McKay—was held in awe even by the shipbuilders themselves. More than any other builder, McKay brought the sharp-bowed, tall-masted sailing ship to perfection.

Like the Tennessean Matthew Fontaine Maury, McKay was farm-bred; in his case, however, the sea had always been a familiar presence. Growing up with 15 brothers and sisters on a marshland farm in Shelburne, Nova Scotia, he breathed salt air and woke to the cry of gulls. With the aid of his younger brother Lauchlan, he built a sailing dinghy and used it for boyhood explorations of Shelburne's bays and the nearby Jordan River. Then, in 1826, 16-year-old Donald rode a coastal schooner from Halifax to New York and got a job as a laborer in an East River shipyard run by Isaac Webb.

Webb has been called the "Father of Shipbuilders" because so many leaders of the industry learned their trade under his tutelage. He was quick to take notice of the young immigrant from Nova Scotia: Right off, McKay showed ability with his tools and a willingness to work from dawn to dusk to learn the shipbuilder's craft. Within a few months McKay and Isaac Webb signed an indenture, apprenticing Donald to Webb "to learn the art, trade and mystery of a ship-carpenter." In return for his lessons, Donald promised his master that he would faithfully serve him, "his secrets keep, his lawful commands everywhere readily obey." The agreement covered virtually all of the young apprentice's waking hours—in fact, it stipulated that "he shall not absent himself day nor night from his master's service without his leave." Nor would he "haunt ale-houses, taverns, dance-houses or playhouses." Besides his tutelage, young McKay would receive $2.50 a week, plus $40 a year "in lieu of meat, drink, washing, lodging, clothing, and other necessaries." The apprenticeship was to last four and a half years.

In fact, it lasted a bit less. After four years of honoring his contract to the letter—by day hefting massive live-oak timbers and straining in the saw pit at one end of a two-handled crosscut saw, by night sticking close to a bachelor boardinghouse aptly nicknamed the "Weary Wanderers' Hotel"—Donald McKay was ready for something new. He had mastered his trade so well that a rival shipbuilder, Jacob Bell, offered him a job as a full-fledged shipwright. He petitioned his master, and Isaac Webb generously released him from his nearly completed apprenticeship.

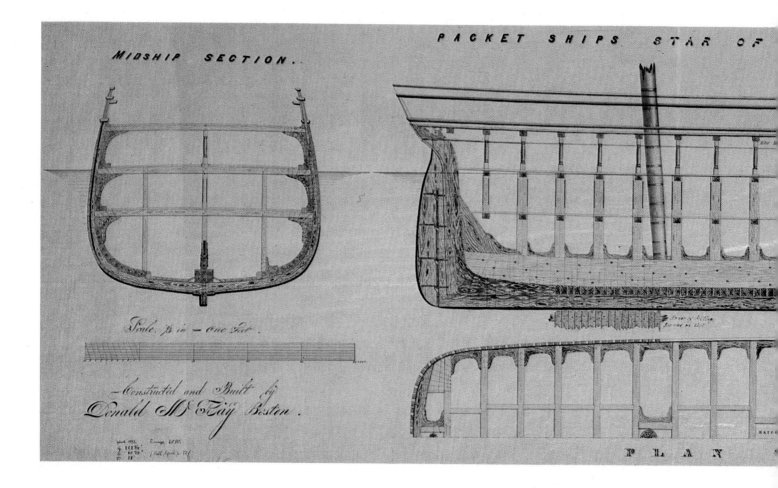

The very next year good fortune favored McKay again: He fell in love with a young lady named Albenia Boole. She was the eldest daughter of John Boole, a successful New York shipbuilder; two of her brothers were shipbuilders as well. Brought up in such a family, Albenia learned to draft and lay off plans as expertly as her brothers. She also had an excellent education, something that Donald had never received.

They were married in 1833. Albenia brought a comfortable dowry to the marriage, and the newlyweds purchased a small house in Manhattan's choice residential area of East Broadway. McKay continued to work for Jacob Bell at the shipyard of Brown & Bell. On Sundays, his one day off, and far into the night on weekdays, he and Albenia sat together in their small parlor while she taught him algebra and trigonometry and filled the many other gaps in his knowledge.

Nearly as important as his marriage was the friendship McKay struck up in the 1830s with John Griffiths, then a draftsman at the nearby Smith & Dimon yard. Long before Griffiths started the shipbuilding revolution with his *Rainbow* and *Sea Witch*, he and McKay had often sat for hours at a drafting board, discussing modifications that might boost the speed of a ship under sail.

All the while, McKay's reputation as a shipwright was growing, and in 1839 he was chosen from a field of nearly a thousand men to become a foreman at the Brooklyn Navy Yard. This triumph, however, soon turned

*Sketched in his own hand, Donald McKay's plans for the twin ships Star of Empire and Chariot of Fame demonstrate his skill in designing for large storage capacity as well as for speed. Although they retained the sleek lines of McKay's more extreme clippers, these three-decked vessels, which were launched in 1853, could carry more cargo in proportion to their registered tonnage than the fullest earlier designs.*

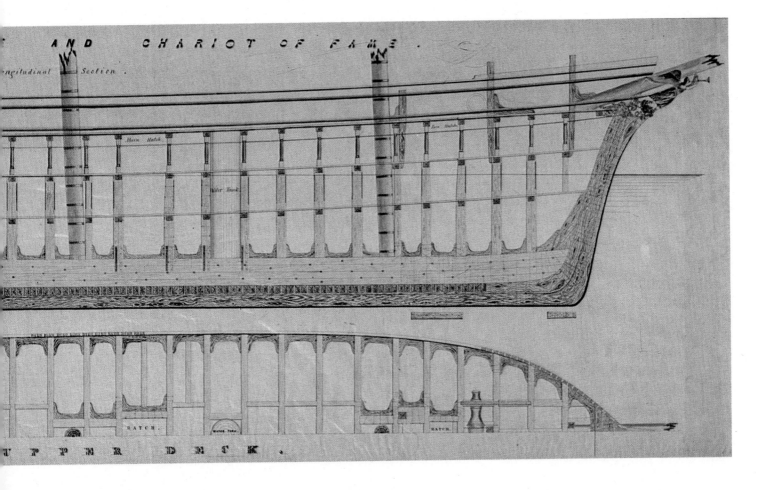

sour. The coincidence of a financial depression and a large influx of immigrants from Europe stirred a ground swell of prejudice in New York against those who were not native-born Americans. The yard hands at the Navy yard refused to work for an immigrant from Nova Scotia. McKay gave up the job and moved to New England, finding employment in Newburyport, Massachusetts, as foreman of a modest-sized shipyard. Once more his gifts were quickly recognized: In 1841 he was offered a partnership by a local shipbuilder named William Currier.

Three years later, after building a series of fine packet ships, McKay was approached by a wealthy Boston merchant named Enoch Train, who offered to set him up with a yard of his own if he would move to Boston. Thus, at the age of 34, Donald McKay was able to test the ideas he and Griffiths had discussed and shaped a decade earlier in New York City.

The first clipper he built in his new shipyard at the foot of Border Street in East Boston was the *Stag Hound,* an extremely narrow vessel that, at the time of her launch in 1850, was the largest merchant ship on the seas. Commissioned by two Boston merchants, she paid for her construction cost in one voyage to California and the Orient, and immediately put McKay in the forefront of clipper builders.

At the first intimations of success, McKay had sent for his wife and children, who had remained behind in Newburyport when he took this new job; he also summoned five of his brothers to come down from Nova Scotia and help him design and build ships. The yard soon seethed with activity. Sawdust, carried by gusts off the harbor, swept across the grounds in clouds. Planking creaked as it was made fast to a vessel's ribs; lumber clattered on the decks; and a steam-powered derrick clanked and hissed as it lifted the heaviest timbers and masts. In other New England yards, timbers were moved about by hand, and all workers left whatever they were doing to help heft a big log into place. McKay's use of a steam hoist, an idea he had brought with him from New York, made this interruption unneccessary, dramatically boosting the shipyard's efficiency. Another McKay innovation was a steam saw that replaced the two-man pit saw. The steam saw saved hours on each job, spared men for other tasks and was more versatile than its man-powered predecessor.

McKay, a curly-haired, brawny man with the brow of a poet and the domineering eye of a bantam rooster, seemed to be everywhere at once—making sure the live oak for a ship's beams had been mature when cut, and had little sap left in it; measuring the impregnation of metallic salts in which the wood had been soaked to guard against dry rot; checking to be sure that the wood had been properly seasoned by drying in the sun; marking a frame with chalk for a sharper curve or a tighter fit; gauging the camber of a newly laid deck to see that it would drain but not be dangerously steep when wet; and supervising the work in hundreds of other ways. The ultimate perfectionist, McKay proclaimed "Excelsior" as the motto for everyone in his yard. "I never yet built a vessel," he claimed, "that came up to my own ideal."

McKay often referred to himself as merely "a mechanic," but he was a great deal more than that: He was, in fact, a brilliant synthesizer. Not an innovative designer himself, he willingly gave credit to men such as John Griffiths for the sharp bow, narrower midships and full stern, and

Nat Palmer for the flatter hull. What McKay did was to take all these improvements in ship design and use them as no one else had.

It was typical of him that, while he was the first shipbuilder in New England to use the newfangled steam hoisting engine and the steam saw, he also employed such venerable tricks as filling narrow tunnels in the keelson with salt pickle to preserve the wood, a technique that had been used in England for years but had rarely been put to work in the United States. McKay simply adopted the finest designs, the newest equipment, the tried and true techniques, and combined them to produce the best clippers ever built.

Early in 1851, before the *Stag Hound* had completed her first voyage, McKay's second clipper, the *Flying Cloud,* was already attracting visitors to the yard. Bostonians came down Border Street to watch her take shape; one onlooker who returned again and again was the poet Henry Wadsworth Longfellow, a devoted ship buff. The great ship's proportions were awesome: 1,783 tons, 229 feet in length, 41 feet in width, 21½ feet in depth. She shouldered aside the *Stag Hound* as the largest merchantman yet built, and she was nearly twice the tonnage of the *Sea Witch,* constructed only five years earlier. The *Flying Cloud* had been commissioned by Enoch Train's firm, and she was, said George Francis Train, cousin and partner of Enoch, a "ship destined to make a new era in shipbuilding all over the world."

Considering their enthusiasm, the Trains now did a curious thing. Among the visitors to McKay's yard were some scouts from the New York shipping firm of Grinnell, Minturn & Co. When they reported on this handsome and promising new clipper, Moses Grinnell promptly offered to buy her, unfinished as she was. And the Trains sold her.

The reason, according to George Train, was that he had responded to Grinnell's offer with what he thought was a very high price, $90,000—and Grinnell, to his surprise, answered, "We will take her." A more likely explanation is that the Train firm found itself short of cash and decided to sell the clipper before she was completed. Whatever the explanation, Enoch Train later confessed that there were few things in his life he regretted more than parting with the *Flying Cloud.*

On April 15, 1851, the crowds poured off the ferry at East Boston all morning. Rowboats and sailboats speckled the harbor, and the McKay yard, the Chelsea Bridge and even the nearby masts and rooftops swarmed with people awaiting the launching. When the dogshores holding her in place were knocked away from the tallow-greased skids, Moses Grinnell's new clipper and Donald McKay's masterpiece eased down the ways, picking up speed and making a thumping splash as she backed into the harbor. Her topmasts had not yet been stepped, but flags flew from the stumps of her lower masts, and long pennants snapped and popped in the brisk spring breeze. The white-and-gold angel that was her figurehead bowed to the onlookers as the big clipper dipped, rolled, righted and glided from the shore. Whistles blew, top hats waved and everyone cheered. That faithful follower of the *Flying Cloud*'s construction, Henry Wadsworth Longfellow, described such an event in one of his poems: "She starts,—she moves,—she seems to feel / The thrill of

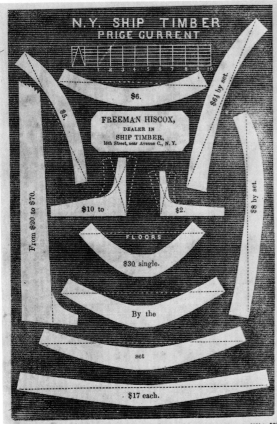

*A timber dealer's advertisement in a magazine for shipbuilders and shipowners reflects the increased standardization of parts as clipper production mushroomed in the mid-1850s. Depending on his pocketbook, a builder had a wide choice of woods—from stout but locally scarce oak to the softer hackmatack, or larch, that grew bountifully all over New England.*

life along her keel,/And, spurning with her foot the ground,/With one exulting, joyous bound,/She leaps into the ocean's arms!''

Several days later, with the truck on her mainmast poking 200 feet into the sky—as high as a 20-story building—and riggers fine-tuning her miles of rigging and shrouds, she set out under tow for New York with her newly appointed commander, Josiah Perkins Creesy, aboard. Creesy had grown up in Marblehead, gone to sea in his teens and become a ship's master at 23. Now 37 and a grizzled veteran of the China trade, he was known as ''Perk'' to his friends—though never to his crew.

For about a month the *Flying Cloud* lay alongside Pier 20 in the East River while her narrow hull was crammed with merchandise for California and while Eleanor Creesy, who always served as her husband's navigator, collected a set of Matthew Maury's *Wind and Current Charts* and *Sailing Directions*. Finally, at 2 p.m. on June 2, 1851, with the white-red-and-blue swallow-tailed flag of Grinnell, Minturn & Co. flying at the masthead, the clipper swung into the river from her pier at the foot of Maiden Lane. She moved slowly through the Narrows, then picked up a fresh afternoon westerly as she approached Sandy Hook.

With a thundering flurry of canvas, her mainsail was backed for a moment. The pilot scampered down the rope ladder and jumped across to the pitching deck of his schooner. The great hull looming above him moved back on course. Her skysails, royals, topgallants, topsails and

## The half-hull model: a designer's three-dimensional sketch pad

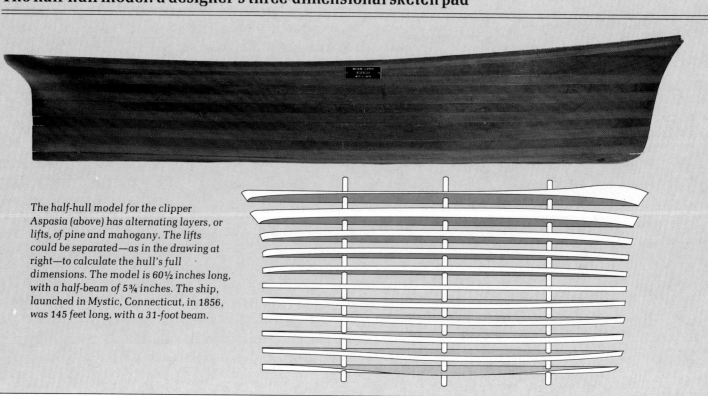

The half-hull model for the clipper *Aspasia* (above) has alternating layers, or lifts, of pine and mahogany. The lifts could be separated—as in the drawing at right—to calculate the hull's full dimensions. The model is 60½ inches long, with a half-beam of 5¾ inches. The ship, launched in Mystic, Connecticut, in 1856, was 145 feet long, with a 31-foot beam.

studding sails boomed, and her masts creaked as she took the wind on her quarter and picked up speed. Twin white waves curled away from her sharp bow, and her rounded stern lifted to the following sea as she went boiling off into the open Atlantic, bound down around Cape Horn to the Golden Gate on a voyage that would never be forgotten.

When the *Flying Cloud* put to sea, the record for the California passage was held by the *Surprise*, an A. A. Low & Bro. clipper that had made the run in 96 days, one day faster than the *Sea Witch's* time over the course. But even on a clipper, the length of the voyage made it, in the words of Matthew Fontaine Maury, "the most tedious within the domains of commerce." Moreover, declared Maury in his elegant style, "many are the vicissitudes which attend it." In particular, Maury observed that the storms along the Gulf Stream are more to be dreaded than those encountered anywhere else in the world. Captain Creesy soon had cause to know why.

June 5, as he laconically recorded in the *Flying Cloud's* log, was a day of "Good breezes, fine weather." But the breezes were out of the northwest and, as breezes out of the northwest frequently do on the Atlantic, they increased to strong winds and finally to a gale. The *Flying Cloud's* towering rigging, as tightly tuned as a giant violin, thrummed and keened as the wind picked up speed. The seas built up into ever-larger hills that marched down on the clipper, lifted her stern and rolled along-

No less eminent a marine architect than John Willis Griffiths called it "a proud emblem of American genius." Donald McKay received praise from a shipwright's publication for being among the first shipbuilders to use it. For all its importance, the object in question—a designer's half-hull model *(left)*—was a simple contrivance that looked like an oversized pull-apart toy. Yet in the hands of men like McKay and Griffiths, it literally gave shape to the clipper-ship era.

The half hull—also referred to as a lift model because its sections could be lifted to separate them—was invented in the 18th Century, but came into widespread use in the 1840s and the 1850s. Before then, the shape of a new vessel's hull was worked out either on paper or in a shipbuilder's head, and translated into wooden reality on the ways, according to his eye.

The models functioned somewhat like a three-dimensional sketch pad, allowing a designer to work out the lineaments of his creation in miniature. The scale of the models varied, but the half hull for a clipper 200 feet long was usually about six feet long. The designer began by stacking together slabs of wood of roughly the right size, securing them with dowels or long triangular wedges. Frequently the wood was pine, or pieces of pine alternating with a darker timber to highlight the lines of the hull.

Using gouges, planes and chisels, the designer sculpted one side of the composite block "to suit his fancy," as a shipwright's manual expressed it. The other side needed no shaping, since it was assumed to be a mirror image of the sculpted half. The completed model was taken apart, and the dimensions of each lift were converted to full size for use in the shipyard.

By the 1870s, shipbuilders found that a hand-carved expression of personal experience and esthetics was an insufficient guide for constructing the new and more complex iron steamships, and precise architectural drafts based on mathematical formulas eventually replaced the designer's model.

Oblivion soon claimed the out-of-date half hulls—in part because designers had been secretive about them. Donald McKay's son noted in a letter that, "owing to jealousy, builders never gave a correct model away." After McKay's death, many of his models were discovered in pieces, chopped up for firewood. Only three escaped destruction, along with a few models by other designers. Apart from a handful of original plans, they are almost all that remains to record the designs of the clipper-ship era.

side; their giant combers toppled forward, and the wind batted off their crests, sweeping the deck with salt spray. Two men fought the huge spoked helm to keep the massive hull from swinging about in each surging sea. Suddenly there was a series of explosive snaps as the elastic hemp supporting the top-hamper stretched and gave way. Within seconds the *Flying Cloud's* main-topgallant mast, and its appended royal and skysail masts, canted to one side. Amid a crackling of wood, the shriek of tearing sails and the clatter of falling blocks, the topgallant mast crashed to the deck in a tangle of shrouds, severing the rigging of the upper mizzenmast as it fell. With its support suddenly gone, the mizzen-topgallant snapped away and fell into the wreckage.

While the mate bellowed orders for all hands to tumble up and take their places on deck, Creesy ordered the helmsman to spin the heavy wheel and let the *Flying Cloud* ease off the wind. Topmen scrambled up the rigging and out onto the yards, some of them barely escaping a plunging death as the main-topsail yard, one of the clipper's longest spars, broke loose and was dragged down by the tangle of the rigging.

Even a partial dismasting of a clipper ship in a gale at sea could make a veteran's blood run cold. The ship swayed to the cross seas. The wind whipped the spars back and forth in murderous parabolas. Blocks swung wildly about like wooden wrecking balls. Gale-driven waves smashed over the bulwarks and washed the men off their feet, sweeping them the width or length of the deck. Some of the wreckage from the top-hamper, still attached to its tangled rigging, had been washed overboard. If these spars and sections of mast were not cut loose, they could drive against the ship's sides like battering rams, smashing through her planking and sinking her. Creesy shouted his orders into the mate's ear; the lines snaking over the rails to the wreckage in the water were chopped away and the remaining rigging was secured. The *Flying Cloud* was eased back on course. Under her reduced canvas, she moved a bit more steadily. And Creesy noted in the log: "Lost Main & Mizen Topgallant mast & Main Topsail yard."

The *Flying Cloud* swept on through a howling night. By late morning the gale had abated somewhat, but the clipper had lost much of her speed. The crew, meanwhile, worked feverishly. With diminishing winds swinging from the northwest into the west and southwest, the topgallant masts and their spars were replaced, new rigging was rove, and lifts were taken aloft as the ship limped on her course southward. The next day the *Cloud's* top-hamper was laboriously hauled back into place. In the space of only 48 hours, the crippled clipper had been restored to racing trim, and by June 8 she was sliding through the rolling seas before a gentle breeze. Creesy wrote in his log, "Fine weather. Set all possible sail."

But evidently those three days had been enough to terrify some of the landlubbers in the crew. Many of them, in fact, were not seamen; some had never been to sea before, and most of the crew had shipped aboard only to get to the gold fields. For the next four days, while the *Flying Cloud* gracefully ran down her easting under gentler breezes, some of the foremast hands relived their nightmare and grumbled among themselves about the greater perils that lay ahead. On June 13 it was discov-

The clipper Flying Cloud takes on cargo in New York shortly before leaving on her maiden voyage to California in June 1851. Though built for fast transport of freight, the vessel was not lacking in amenities for her few passengers. A New York newspaper said it knew of no packet ship or steamer more luxurious.

ered that the clipper's mainmast was, as Creesy recorded, "badly sprung about a foot from the Hound"—that is, twisted and partially fractured at the junction where the topgallant mast had wrenched away from it. And three days later, when the winds picked up again and blustery squalls swept down on them, the men eyed the bending, creaking main-topmast with undisguised anxiety. The Flying Cloud's top-hamper stood up under the buffeting, but the experience only added to the crew's concern.

By June 19 the Cloud was entering the doldrums, heralded by intermittent squalls and periods when the sea was as smooth as a millpond, and the ship's progress under sail was frustratingly meager. In the captain's cabin, Mrs. Creesy opened Matthew Maury's book on her chart table and plotted a course through the region. By June 21 her husband was showing his first sign of impatience: His cryptic, unemotional observations in the log gave way to a complaining "Calm Calm Calm." But by the morning of June 23 the log was reporting fresh squalls, and by late afternoon the *Cloud* was once again experiencing "Gentle breezes" and "fine weather." With Maury's guidance, Mrs. Creesy had brought the ship through this navigational slough in only four days.

Shortly before midnight on June 24, the *Flying Cloud* slipped across the Equator, only 22 days out of New York, and bent her course southward. By June 26 the clipper had made enough easting to round the bulge of Cape São Roque. And now the mood aboard became more ominous. Instead of heading for Rio de Janeiro and repairs for the injured mast, Creesy set course for Cape Horn, where rocky islands curled out eastward from under the continent like a finger beckoning malevolently to oncoming ships. If a mid-Atlantic gale had carried away the ship's top-hamper, might not "Cape Stiff," as the Horn was unlovingly called by seamen, with its murderous gales and blasting snowstorms, strip her as clean as an Indian canoe? So the greener members of the crew must have reasoned. And even the least imaginative foremast hand, after experiencing the partial dismasting three weeks earlier, could visualize the disaster that might occur if the entire mainmast went over the side. But the *Cloud* had begun to pick up the Southern Hemisphere's southeast trade winds, and now nothing short of a mutiny could have persuaded Creesy to put into port.

On July 9 the wind increased to a fresh breeze. That morning, before dawn, a brief thunderstorm flashed across the Atlantic, flattening the waves with its downpour and leaving sparkling whitecaps in its wake. These were weather-breeding conditions and, as the inexperienced crew grew more mistrustful, Creesy braced himself for the storm that finally struck later that day.

It started with another thunderstorm, this one violent. Because Cressy had seen it coming, he had time to order skysails, royals and topgallants furled and the topsails double-reefed, cutting down their exposed surface area by about a third. The storm kept up all that night, and morning brought even stronger winds. In his log Creesy noted "blowing hard Gale—No Observations." He ordered the topsails shortened to their last rows of reef points. All the clipper carried now were close-reefed topsails and staysails—fore-and-aft triangles of canvas rigged between the masts and intended to help steady the ship as she ran before the storm. But even these were strained mightily by the wind, and suddenly, with a great ripping sound, two of her staysails split into tatters. Rushing and sliding about the water-washed decks, the men lowered and gathered in the remnants and stowed them below. While they were working they could hear a groaning, cracking noise: The weakened masthead was threatening to give way.

Creesy looked off to leeward and saw that the *Cloud* had company. Not far away a brig was laboring desperately. As he watched, her fore- and main-topmasts canted over, split away and tumbled into the sea. With his own mainmast bending and creaking, Creesy was too busy to go to her aid. He ordered his upper yards lowered in an attempt to ease the strain on the mast. The clipper was dipping the tips of her yardarms into the sea as she rolled to leeward. Water rushed over the lee rail and swept waist-high across the deck, knocking men off their feet and sending them thumping against the deck housing. But one by one the spars were

# Enchanting relics of a lost nautical art

Although they are remembered chiefly as a streamlined embodiment of sheer speed, clippers were also the last great seafaring home of a major decorative art: the craftwork of the ship carver.

Ship carving dates back to the beginnings of maritime history. Small carvings—often a stylized eye believed to possess supernatural powers of guidance—appeared on the bows of Egyptian ships even before 1000 B.C. More elaborate figureheads, usually swans or horses, later adorned Phoenician and Roman vessels. But the zenith of this art form was achieved on the magnificent wooden sailing ships of the 19th Century.

The master ship carvers of the day practiced their work on a variety of shipboard subjects, including figureheads, nameboards, billetheads, transoms and binnacles *(right)*. On clipper ships—in keeping with pioneer designer John W. Griffiths' conviction that "the head of a ship stamps an impression on the mind in relation to the entire ship"—figureheads such as the ones on the following pages provided the bulk of the carvers' commissions.

Most figureheads straightforwardly reflected the names of the clippers they graced—a simple matter in cases like *Carrier Pigeon*, *Game Cock* and *Stag Hound*. But at times a carver was hard-pressed to suitably represent the name of a ship. The *Charmer* sported what one observer—making an unkind reference to a Boston reservoir—described as "a snake with the tongue hanging out as if it had a drink of Cochituate water and did not like it."

Clearly, the best of the ship carvers' creations were their human figures. Most often the figures were female—appreciatively characterized by Joseph Conrad as "women with mural crowns, women with flowing robes, stretching out rounded arms as if to point the way."

For the ship carvers themselves, the road ahead was anything but promising. As the construction of wooden vessels declined, more and more carvers closed their doors and put away their shop-front notices such as the one below. By 1896, when this sign was removed from the entranceway of the Boston firm of Hastings & Gleason, an ancient craft had all but disappeared from the seafarers' world.

*This binnacle boy—with an injunction to "mind your helm" inscribed on his hat—carried the clipper N. B. Palmer's compass inside its brass binnacle. So lifelike was the figure that strange tales about its power circulated on the Palmer. Helmsmen insisted that it was haunted and that the boy's eyes followed them. Their fear eventually led to the removal of the figure from the ship.*

*Carved in 1839, this sign served five Boston firms in succession during the next 57 years.*

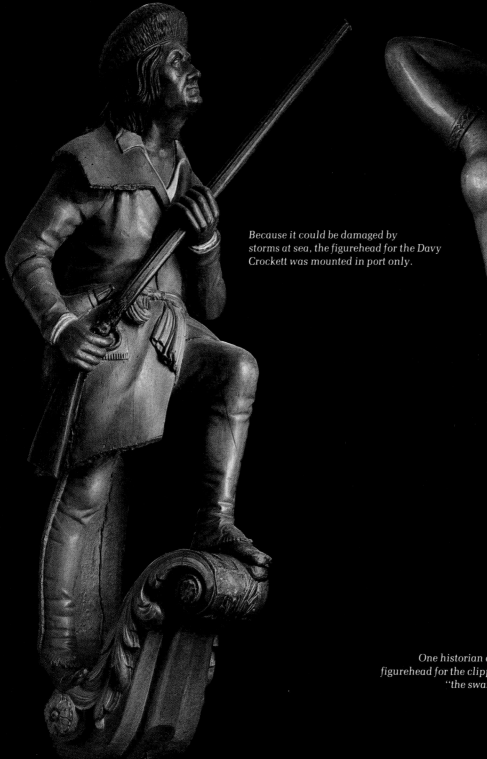

Because it could be damaged by storms at sea, the figurehead for the Davy Crockett was mounted in port only.

One historian called this classical figurehead for the clipper Glory of the Sea "the swan song of the craft."

The figurehead carved for the Great Republic was removed after a fire almost destroyed the clipper in 1853.

Carrying a claymore, a Scottish sword, this Highlander graced the clipper Donald McKay, named for her designer.

A rendering of Galatea, a star-crossed sea nymph in Greek mythology, adorned the bow of the ship of that name.

brought down, first the royal and then the topgallant yards. The main-mast seemed firmer without their weight. But the gale continued to increase, in periodic, thundering gusts.

It continued through another night. In such weather the clipper's sharp bow no longer sliced through the waves. The seas had grown so large that the *Cloud* would race downhill as one wave rose astern, then rise as the moving mountain went under her. Atop the peak of the giant wave, her masts would shudder and her thin row of reefed sail would slat violently. Then down again, so deep in the trough that her sails would go limp. All night long the clipper lurched and heaved as the phosphorescent surf exploded all around her.

The storm raged on through the morning of the next day, and early that afternoon Creesy was told that his ship was leaking. The forecastle, positioned atop the main deck on the *Flying Cloud*, was already awash with much more water than could have come in from the deck, and it was getting ahead of the pumps. Bellowing to each other on the afterdeck, Creesy and the ship's carpenter analyzed the situation. The carpenter thought that the stopper in the anchor hawsehole to port had been forced out and that the water could be entering there. Creesy barked at the helmsman. The *Flying Cloud* eased off the wind slightly and righted a bit while the carpenter went to inspect the hawsehole. A few moments later he came racing aft to report that the *Cloud* had been sabotaged.

The hawsehole stopper had indeed come loose. But after repairing it, the carpenter saw that the water, instead of draining overboard through the scuppers, was pouring into the 'tween decks through a hole beneath an after bunk. As he tried to stopper it, he discovered that some-one had made it by drilling two auger holes through the ship's deck and using a marlinespike to join the two into a single opening four inches across. The sea poured through it into the under decks and hold, soaking some of the cargo and threatening to swamp the ship.

Creesy put the clipper back on course. As the storm tore at her scant sails and the crew heaved at the pumps, the carpenter and his helpers worked to plug the leak. Creesy meanwhile ordered the mate to find the culprit. It did not take long; the man had been foolish enough to drill the holes under his own bunk, hoping, no doubt, to force the *Cloud* into port. And another crew member reported seeing him emerging from the fore-castle with an auger in his hand. It was also discovered that the saboteur had had an accomplice. Both men were seized and put into irons.

Meanwhile, the carpenter's ministrations proved successful: The fore-castle was soon pumped out and the *Flying Cloud* continued her plunging course southward. By the time the gale finally moderated the next day, the clipper's deck was a mass of splintered railings and gear. There was so much repair work and cleanup to be done that Creesy had the irons taken off the two saboteurs long enough for them to help.

On July 19, dainty storm petrels and great wheeling albatrosses appeared in the sky overhead, indicating that the *Flying Cloud* was approaching Cape Horn. That afternoon the wind gradually veered into the northeast and picked up strength once again. Creesy had to order the studding sails taken in before their booms dipped into the water and were carried away.

*Fiery New Englander Josiah P. Creesy was chosen to be the Flying Cloud's first commander in 1851 on the basis of his reputation for getting peak performance from his ships and crews. In four years at the helm, Creesy more than justified his selection: He made five runs from New York to California in an average time of just over 100 days, and twice made the voyage in a breakneck 89 days, a record that was never surpassed under sail.*

The next morning Mrs. Creesy, her arms hugging the sides of her swaying chart table, told her husband that they had better alter course. By her calculations, the point of Cape San Diego lay dead ahead, and the weather was too thick to sight the land in time to wear off. The rain that had come on with the northerly wind had turned to sleet and was rapidly developing into a blizzard. Creesy sent the *Cloud* northward, away from the rocky cape, and called for furled courses; however, he left the topsails up, close-reefed so that, as the ship sank into the valleys between the huge waves, these upper sails would hold the wind and keep the ship under way and maneuverable.

The *Cloud* was fairly in Cape Horn weather now. The snowstorm continued throughout the 20th as the ship zigzagged back to the south. The wind drove the snow across the deck in nearly horizontal sheets, piling drifts on the leeward sides of the deckhouses. The next day the temperature moderated a bit and the snow turned to rain. But, as Creesy noted, there was a "bad sea Running" and the *Cloud* was shipping water across her deck. Then, on July 22, the skies cleared. Ten miles off her starboard bow stood Cape San Diego, a black band of granite over the slate-gray sea. Mrs. Creesy's dead-reckoning navigation was exactly on target.

In moderated winds, the *Flying Cloud* ran through the Strait of Le Maire, between Cape San Diego and Staten Island, with all sails set. By 6 p.m. she was safely through and in open water, with the land out of sight. A strong tide was setting northward, and Creesy posted a lookout in the bow to keep watch for ship-crushing formations of drifting ice. Next morning the wind was light; Creesy ordered all sails set again. And at 8 a.m. there it was: Cape Horn, only five miles north of them.

The snow-covered, 1,391-foot headland fell away to a white-blanketed shore. Swirling clouds of ducks swept in moving patterns over the bleak promontory, swinging down and splash-landing near the rocks. As the sailors watched, another snow squall raced toward them. Cape Horn disappeared behind a white curtain, and the *Cloud* raced on westward toward the Pacific. Mrs. Creesy, with the aid of Maury's charts, had navigated the clipper so well that she had not gone much farther south than 56°, well north of the course that most ships took around the Horn. By noon of July 26 the *Cloud* was at lat. 50.57°, romping up the western coast of South America in a fine breeze under clear skies. Her transit of the Horn had been remarkably swift. Many ships spent weeks and sometimes even months making good the same distance that she had covered in just three days.

Before facing the Horn, Creesy had lowered the topgallant and royal yards to relieve the weakened mainmast; now, with the weather improved, he sent them up again. For four days the winds continued moderate, with only an occasional light rain squall, and by July 30 the *Cloud* was more than 1,000 miles up the coast at 41° 58′ S., with all studding sails drawing and a fresh southeasterly on her starboard quarter. But late that afternoon the wind became squally. Creesy brought in some of the studding sails. The wind soon piped up to storm strength, and by 2 a.m. of July 31 the *Cloud* was staggering under a series of sharp squalls. At dawn everyone was eying the weakened mainmast again.

Creesy decided to chance leaving the topgallants set this time to see

*Josiah Creesy used this 17-inch-long brass speaking trumpet to shout orders to crewmen high in the rigging or to hail nearby vessels amid stormy seas. The instrument is inscribed with the captain's name just above its flared bell.*

what she could do. He stood spread-legged on his slanting quarter-deck and watched his fine ship leap ahead before each smashing squall. A mate and his crew, hanging onto the lee rail, logged the *Cloud's* speed. One man tossed a weighted piece of wood called a drogue over the side; another watched a sandglass as the line attached to the drogue flew off its drum. The line was marked at intervals to measure the amount yanked out after the drogue. Creesy and his men were dumfounded to see the line play itself out entirely before all the sand had passed through the glass. This meant that the *Flying Cloud* was traveling at a speed somewhere in excess of 18 knots. At first they could not believe it, but when Mrs. Creesy calculated their noon-to-noon run from her sextant observations she found that the *Flying Cloud* had run 374 nautical miles, an average speed of about 15½ knots. No sailing ship had ever before attained this speed. Other clippers would soon go still faster, but almost a quarter of a century would pass before any steamship could match the pace of the *Flying Cloud.*

Streaking for the Golden Gate, her gilt-and-white angel clipping through the wave tops like a dolphin, the *Cloud* raced on through more squalls. Finally, to spare his groaning mainmast, Creesy ordered the topgallants taken in, and double-reefed the fore- and mizzen-topsails.

*Carrying only her topsails and a small jib in a violent gale, the Flying Cloud scuds past Cape Horn in this oil by 19th Century marine painter J. E. Buttersworth. The topsails—low enough for easy reefing but still high enough to catch the wind when the ship was in the trough of a wave—enabled the vessel to hold her course in a storm without overtaxing the masts and rigging.*

The clipper scarcely slowed, making 334 miles on the next day's run.

On August 12 the *Flying Cloud* raced past the Equator and into north latitudes. The northeast trades took over, fresh and full. Creesy kept everything flying; he knew by now that he stood a chance of breaking the *Surprise's* record of 96 days. For the next 12 days he was blessed with favorable winds and relatively clear weather, and the *Cloud* devoured her route with runs averaging better than 200 miles a day. On August 24 the wind dropped, and the next two days brought an agonizing succession of "Light Baffling" breezes, as Creesy described them. Then the fresh winds returned, followed on August 29 by squalls. Racing for a record, Creesy kept his lofty sails flying—and lost his fore-topgallant mast.

But he refused to give up now. And most of his previously disaffected crew had also caught the fever. With superhuman effort, despite more shrieking squalls, they got the topgallant mast back in place in only 24 hours. Then, on August 31, Creesy recorded: "At 6 AM made South Farallone." The Farallon Islands mark the entrance to San Francisco harbor. Running for the finish line with a squally northwester on her weather bow and with everything flying except Perk Creesy's nightshirt, the *Flying Cloud* swooped down on the Golden Gate. She pulled up briefly before entering San Francisco Bay, and a pilot came aboard to guide her to her dock.

Most of Captain Creesy's crew immediately deserted and swarmed through the city's saloons on their way to the gold fields. As a result, within hours everyone in San Francisco had heard the news: Donald McKay's amazing new clipper had made the passage from New York to the Golden Gate in 89 days 21 hours, bettering the time of the *Surprise* by nearly a week.

After selling his cargo of cheese, butter and other goods prized in that brash but remote metropolis, Creesy put to sea again, racing on around the world, across the Pacific to Canton, then around the Cape of Good Hope and on to New York with a fresh crop of tea. There, Creesy and the *Cloud* received a riotous welcome. Newspapers called the voyage a national triumph. "The log of the *Flying Cloud* is now before us," wrote one editor. "It is the most wonderful record that pen ever indited, for rapid as was the passage, it was performed under circumstances by no means the most favorable."

The *Flying Cloud* had paid for herself on this one round-the-world voyage, and the grateful Messrs. Grinnell and Minturn had her log printed in gold letters on white silk, making a number of copies to distribute to friends of the firm in the hope that they would remember the feat the next time the *Flying Cloud* loaded for California.

In the years that followed the *Flying Cloud's* legendary run to San Francisco, more and more clipper ships came down the runways of shipyards from Maine to Virginia and struck off around the Horn with lucrative cargoes for the California market. In many cases, they sailed on from San Francisco to China, where they took on cargoes of tea—often destined not for the Americans but for the tea-thirsty British.

Only a few years earlier, that trade would have been closed to Ameri-

While a pilot schooner bobs in the foreground, the Flying Cloud (far left) and the steamer John L. Stephens converge on San Francisco Bay in this 1855 lithograph. Both clipper ships and paddle-wheelers prospered on the run to California.

Steamship lines charged passengers $600 first-class and $300 steerage for a five-week trip from New York via Panama; clippers, whose chief business was freight, usually took about four months by way of Cape Horn and charged passengers a flat $300.

can ships by the British Navigation Acts, laws that since the time of Oliver Cromwell had, in effect, assured a monopoly for British ships in trade between the British Isles and the Orient. The British East India Company, a gigantic quasi-governmental trading institution, had grown fat and rich as its vessels made their ponderous way out to Asian ports of call and back to London. Until the early 1800s, they often had taken a year or a year and a half each way. On such voyages two to three knots was the average rate of speed, all light sails were taken in at sundown, and if there was the merest suggestion of bad weather the ship hove to for the night. During the first half of the 19th Century, competition with other British ships caused the stately East Indiamen to speed up their runs to the Orient, but they still lagged considerably behind the swifter vessels from the United States.

Fortunately for the British merchant marine, Parliament foresaw that eventual economic isolation would be the consequence of the Navigation Acts. In 1849 Parliament repealed them, in the hope that British merchants would be stimulated to construct faster vessels that could compete with the trading vessels of other nations—particularly the speedy American clippers.

Parliament did not have to wait long for its plan to work. In August 1850 an American clipper arrived in Hong Kong to take on tea for London. The ship was the *Oriental*, under the command of Nat Palmer's brother Ted, and she was one of the fastest vessels in the American merchant fleet at that time. On her voyage out to Hong Kong from New York she had broken the record for the route, running it in 81 days. With this stunning accomplishment to recommend her, British shippers in Hong Kong competed for space in her holds. The East Indiamen had been loading tea at freight rates of 3 pounds 10 shillings per 50 cubic feet. Palmer took on a cargo of fresh tea at the unheard-of rate of six pounds per 40 cubic feet. Crammed to her bulkheads with 1,600 tons of the precious crop, the *Oriental* raised anchor and slid out of Hong Kong harbor on August 28, 1850. In 97 days she was in London.

The arrival of the *Oriental* caused a sensation in Victorian London. Crowds flocked to the West India Dock to inspect this tall newcomer. They commented on her sharp bow and her long, slim hull, and pointed to her soaring skysail yards. The British had built some ships larger than the *Oriental*, but none with such towering masts, which seemed to rise like redwoods in a forest of oak. The *Oriental* lorded it over every ship in the harbor, many of whose boats drifted alongside her, oars dripping while the mariners in them shook their heads in disbelief. Palmer saw to it that every sail was furled tight as a drumhead, every bit of brightwork polished, every line coiled in place.

London's countinghouses buzzed with envious comment and dire predictions. Now that England's merchant fleet was no longer protected by the Navigation Acts, the United States of America, only 74 years old, bade fair to dominate her parent country's tea trade just as surely as this big clipper dominated the British ships in the Thames. "The Thunderer," as *The Times* of London was known, thundered: "We must run a race with our gigantic and unshackled rival. We must set our long-practised skill, our steady industry, and our dogged determination,

The Oriental, first U.S. clipper to carry tea from China to England after the repeal of British statutes that restricted the trade to British vessels, approaches the West India Dock in London on December 3, 1850. The Oriental's arrival, wrote a chronicler of the clipper era, "aroused almost as much apprehension and excitement in Great Britain as was created by the memorable Tea Party held in Boston harbor in 1773."

against his youth, ingenuity, and ardor. It is a father who runs a race with his son. A fell necessity constrains us and we must not be beat. Let our ship-builders and employers take warning in time."

They did. Before the *Oriental* dropped down the Thames to return to China, the Admiralty requested permission to take off her lines, and she was towed to the dry dock at Blackwall to provide example and inspiration for local shipbuilders. In short order, the British had begun to produce vessels that could challenge the American monopoly on speed under sail. Their clippers were smaller than the Yankee ships designed to sail around Cape Horn, but they were well suited to the China run in that they had a narrower beam that made them faster and more weatherly in the light breezes of the Indian Ocean.

Thus, within two years of the *Sea Witch's* startling Hong Kong-to-New York run of 1849, the clipper had become established as the most desirable ship for long-haul voyages to any corner of the globe. Shipyards in Britain and the United States were building clippers as fast as they could, and merchants everywhere gladly paid the clippers' higher freight rates. The shippers were buying speed and, as more and more clippers competed for their business, clipper captains drove their ships and their crews to the limit to see that the customer got what he was paying for.

# From mold loft to launch: genesis of a Yankee clipper

Building a clipper involved a measure of intuition, since no two clipper hulls were exactly alike: Each was a fresh attempt to create the perfect sailing ship. The designer first sculpted a model of the hull (below and pages 56-57), whose curves could be enlarged and outlined in the mold loft (right) to produce templates for shaping the timbers.

If the clipper had been commissioned from a small shipyard like the one pictured on these pages, the various woods—rock maple and white oak from Massachusetts, cedar and pine from Maine, live oak from the South—were often cut specifically for that ship (big yards usually stockpiled timber so that construction could begin as soon as orders were received). The trees were felled during the winter months, when most of their rot-inducing sap had fallen into the roots and lower trunk. In the spring, to hurry the seasoning, the timbers were stripped of bark, steeped in hot water to remove the remaining sap and dried in the sun.

Over the following months, teams of craftsmen—carpenters, dubbers, joiners, calkers and fasteners—worked together to translate the designer's vision into reality. Timbers were sculpted into structural elements and adzed smooth. Thousands of wooden fasteners called treenails (but pronounced "trunnels") were split by hand to within a fraction of the standard inch-and-a-quarter diameter. And planks were steamed in ovens until they were pliable enough to be bent into the requisite hull contours. Gradually the new clipper rose on its bed of keelblocks by the river's edge, where, less than a year after the order for the ship was placed, it finally reached completion.

*With a mallet and a gouge, a designer shapes his model (below) before taking it to the mold loft (right). There, the model's contours—enlarged to full size—are traced on the floor with chalk; flexible battens, temporarily pinned to the floor, guide the tracing and ensure smooth curves. The chalk lines, in turn, are guides for making wooden templates, which will be used as patterns for the ship's ribs.*

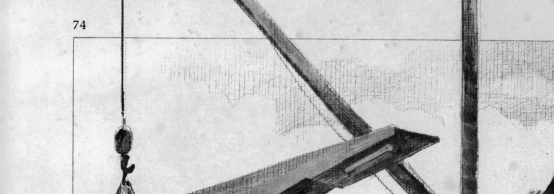

A horse-powered derrick lowers one of
the massive white-oak timbers that make
the clipper's keel—the backbone of the
hull. Two men guide the timber so that the
butt, which has been cut on a stepped
diagonal, will form a snug joint with the
piece that is already in place on the
keelblocks. This junction, called a hook-
scarf joint, will then be clenched with
yard-long iron pins, known as driftbolts.

On a platform built out on either side
of the keel, the ship's frames, or ribs, are
assembled from sections that have
been hewn to match the curves of the
mold-loft templates. One by one, the
gigantic horseshoe-shaped ribs are hoisted
upright and fitted onto the keel.
Once they are up, the keelson—another
composite of joined timbers—is bolted
along the hull's center line, sandwiching
the frames tightly against the keel.

On scaffolding that has been built up alongside the hull, a dubber (left) uses an adz to flatten sections of the curve of a frame so that the planking—some of it nearly seven inches thick—will sit snugly in place. Working with a big auger, a borer (right) drills holes through each plank and into the frames behind. A mallet man follows him, securing the planks by pounding hardwood treenails into each drill hole. Later, another yard hand will saw each treenail off flush with the side of the ship.

With the deck beams installed, three yard hands support a structural element called a knee, while a fourth worker pounds a heavy lumber prop to wedge the knee firmly in position. A fifth man (left) drives driftbolts through another knee to hold it. Knees, each cut from a single piece of wood, reinforced the joints where the deck beams met the frames. Each beam had a hanging knee set under it and a lodging knee on each side.

A team of calkers seals the deck with oakum and tar. Two men (background, left and right) force strands of tar-soaked hemp—the oakum—between the planks. Another calker holds a long-handled hawsing iron while a mallet man strikes the head of the iron to drive the oakum into the cracks; his tool, called a hawsing beetle, made a distinctive "boink" sound. Behind them a fifth worker pours hot tar into the seams as a final seal.

To start the vessel down the ways at the launch, a pair of yard hands smash the blocks of wood that support the keel. As the blocks are knocked away, the weight of the hull is thrown onto the cradles—piles of beams built up along the hull's underbelly. An interface between two layers of the cradle beams has been greased and, as the weight settles onto the cradles, the top layer begins to slip, letting the ship move down the incline and into the water.

With a clatter of tumbling keelblocks and a tremendous splash, the new vessel enters the water stern first. Temporary braces keep her rudder from swinging to one side and breaking off. The clipper's designer and some of her owners ride on her deck, eager to see how she will take to her element. Following the launch festivities, she will be towed to a rigger's wharf and fitted out with the miles of rigging that will support her permanent masts, yards and sails.

# Chapter 3

# Behind the romance, a bitter test of wills

uly 13, 1851, was a day of great anticipation on the New York City waterfront: A new clipper ship, the *Challenge*, was about to set off on her maiden voyage. Sailing day for a clipper was always a special event, but the *Challenge* caused even more of a stir than most ships. At 2,006 tons, with a 230-foot mainmast and an astonishing 12,780 square yards of sail, she was the largest and the most imposing clipper ever built up to that time. And she was to be commanded by the celebrated Robert "Bully" Waterman, former captain of the first true clipper, the *Sea Witch*, the ship that had stunned the world by speeding from China to New York in 74 days in 1849.

At 43, Bully Waterman was a rich man, thanks to his years with the *Sea Witch* and, before that, with the packet *Natchez*. He had been intending to retire and enjoy his wealth ashore, but the shipping firm of N. L. & G. Griswold (a company so successful that rivals said the initials stood for "No Loss and Great Gain") induced him to take command of the *Challenge* by promising him a bonus of $10,000 if he got her to San Francisco in 90 days—a mark no one had achieved, although the *Flying Cloud* was even then in the process of setting her record of 89 days and 21 hours. Almost as irresistible as the bonus was the opportunity to drive an untried vessel—a temptation for any captain.

Now, on this summer's day seven weeks after a gala launching that had drawn bigger crowds than any other in New York memory, a skeleton crew aboard the *Challenge* cast off her lines and took her down the East River to a position near Battery Park at the foot of Manhattan Island. There she paused, riding at anchor while harbor taxis ferried out four passengers and the rest of her full complement: the captain and three mates, 56 crewmen and eight cabin boys.

On the banks of Battery Park and aboard small craft bobbing in the harbor, spectators awaited a glimpse of the captain. Bob Waterman, having a flair for the dramatic, was the last to arrive—and he made his entrance in style. Dressed for the occasion in a tall beaver hat, frock coat and trousers pressed razor-sharp, he stood in the stern of the boat that rowed him briskly through the milling dinghies and dories. Spotting him, the onlookers sent up a cheer. The captain raised his topper to return the salute, then climbed smartly up the rope ladder and onto the quarter-deck of the *Challenge*. His mate was waiting for him. "All right, Mister! A man for the wheel," the captain announced in a voice loud enough to carry to his floating audience. "Give me a jib and a foretops'l."

Nimble-footed men swarmed up the rigging and out along the spars. The sails unrolled like enormous white wings. The windlass clanked as

*A thicket of rigging rises above vessels awaiting loading at New York's East River wharves in the 1860s. Setting off from here, clipper masters mercilessly pressed their ships and crews to achieve record-breaking runs. "She was built for hard usage," said one captain of his clipper, "and I intended she should do her duty."*

the anchor inched up from the water, and the chanteyman helped along the labor by singing out the rhythmic lines of a familiar sailor's air (a favorite on such occasions was "A bully ship and a bully crew," with the crewmen grunting in chorus as they leaned into the capstan bars, "Doo-dah! Doo-dah!"). Her anchor dripping at the cathead, her wide sails set before the breeze, the *Challenge* gathered way and moved grandly down the bay as the audience shouted final cheers of farewell.

If the sailing was an inspiring occasion for those looking on, it was something quite different for those aboard. Most of the men moving at the capstan to the chanteyman's call were drunk and staggering, and most of their shipmates still lay unconscious and stinking of booze in the berths where they had been dumped after being helped or carried aboard. Only a few of the men adroitly scampering about the rigging were in fact members of the crew; the majority were longshoremen brought aboard for the occasion, and as soon as the ship began to move they went over the side into waiting boats and were rowed back to shore.

Nor was the captain exactly the gentlemanly figure that he had seemed to be when boarding the ship. The precise details of what happened on board as the *Challenge* was leaving port are not known. But if Waterman

*Spectators at William Webb's East River shipyard cheer the Challenge—the first three-decked clipper built in America and the largest merchantman of her day—as she slips from the ways on May 24, 1851. "End or broadside on, her appearance is truly beautiful," said an observer. "If cast in a mould she could not have been more perfect to the eye."*

was following his usual practice, he had the sailors assembled on deck—as soon as they could be roused—to witness a strange, symbolic ritual. He called for a bucket of sea water and splashed his own face with it—a gesture designed to convey that he was washing away his shore self and assuming a different persona for life at sea. It is known that on this day, surveying the sorry lot who would crew the *Challenge*, he muttered, "I'll make sailors of 'em, or else mincemeat." He was not long in underlining his intention with action. Before the *Challenge* was out of New York Harbor, Waterman rebuked a black steward for some unrecorded offense by bloodying the man's scalp with a carving knife.

For the watchers ashore, a graceful clipper was winging toward romance and adventure. For the men on board ship, a hellish voyage was getting under way.

The *Challenge* was by no means unique in this Jekyll-and-Hyde contrast. As it happened, the voyage on which she set off that day in 1851 would engender particularly lasting notoriety, because the brutal events that ensued would later be held up for examination in court and in the press. Similar incidents, however—different not in character but only in degree and in being concealed from public notice—were the common stuff of clipper voyages. Many—probably most—clipper passages were bitter contests of wills between surly crews who were being compelled to do difficult, dangerous work for which many of them had no skills or special liking, and captains who were determined to get their vessels to their destinations as rapidly as possible, however hard that might be on the sailors. To some extent, the same could be said of any ships of the era. But because clipper owners and masters put such emphasis on speed and therefore were so much more demanding of their vessels and their crews, the animosities and harshness that plagued merchant shipping in general were greatly intensified aboard clippers.

A major cause of this endemic conflict was a shortage of skilled seamen. Only a generation or two earlier, every ambitious lad in the northeastern United States had wanted to go to sea. In 1805, for one striking example, 20 young men from Harvard volunteered as ordinary seamen aboard the merchant ship *America*. A dozen years later, a follow-up study revealed that 19 of the 20 had become captains (the 20th had disappeared). Such a prodigality of manpower was seen no more. The opportunities of the opening West were an increasing attraction. So were the growing number of factory jobs—providing better pay and more freedom than life at sea, even if the factory worker labored from 5 a.m. until well into the night six days a week.

In the decade since 1840, the demand for seamen had grown while the supply had diminished: The total tonnage of all United States merchant sailing ships had risen from 900,000 to 1.5 million, and oceangoing steamer tonnage had gone from zero to 45,000. Given the preference of Americans for jobs ashore and the strength of the young nation's economy, American clippers had to be crewed largely by foreigners. As often as not, they were the dregs of Europe's waterfront dives.

Moreover, these newcomers were also deserting for the West, responding to the same lure that had drawn off so many other Americans:

California gold and the boom that it generated. Some of the more responsible captains attempted to point out to the shipowners that $12 a month for the man-killing work aboard a clipper could hardly compete with the then princely wages of $50 a week that were being offered in the shops and saloons of San Francisco. But the shipowners, perhaps realizing that they could not hope to match such sums, refused to offer any more money for foremast hands.

Inevitably they turned to the crimp, who virtually kidnapped the derelicts off waterfronts everywhere and delivered them to ships in exchange for an advance on the man's pay. Nor were derelicts the only victims: A seaman newly returned from a voyage would saunter into the nearest bar or brothel, and next day find himself awaking from a stupor aboard another ship. Often the stupor was induced by drugs in his drink. An inventive method was employed by one San Francisco saloon operator who called herself Miss Piggott. She offered her clientele a doped drink (referred to by the knowledgeable as a Miss Piggott Special) at a bar in front of which was a trap door. A crimp easily scooped up the drugged sailor-to-be in the basement.

The captains had no choice but to contract with these providers, since there was no other way to man their ships. They did object to the frequent substitution of corpses, and to other unfair tactics—for example, the practice of one San Francisco crimp known as Nikko the Lapp, who often delivered dummies cleverly made of sailor's gear stuffed with straw; he sometimes inserted a few rats in a dummy's arm to make it twitch like that of a man in a drunken sleep.

Few crews included more than half a dozen able-bodied seamen who had voluntarily signed on; most of the rest of a typical crew of 50 or more were victims of the vicious crimping dragnet. No man along the waterfront in the United States was entirely safe. A poignant instance was that of a ship captain who overindulged while in a New Orleans saloon and subsequently woke up in the forecastle of a strange ship; luckily, he was able to prove his identity before the vessel sailed.

Understandably, the men recruited in this manner did not often make willing, eager, obedient sailors—although they were generally sturdy enough. Merchant captain Samuel Samuels declared that seamen of that era were "the toughest class of men in all respects. They could stand the worst weather, food and usage." But, he added, "they had not the slightest idea of morality or honesty, and gratitude was not in them. The dread of the belaying-pin or heaver"—a heaver was a tarred, knotted rope that officers used like a billy club—"kept them in subjection. I tried to humanize these brutal natures as much as possible, but the better they were treated the more trouble my officers had with them."

The clipper captain had to be even tougher than the men if he hoped to forge a serviceable crew out of kidnapped landlubbers and a few experienced but rebellious seamen. And to wrest optimum performances from both crew and ship, he also had to be knowledgeable and single-minded. For three or four months, without a moment's letup day or night, he was under unremitting tension, since the success or failure of the voyage was entirely on his shoulders. He had to keep the clipper flying every possible square foot of sail, judging what she would carry by such arcane

*Drunken seamen topple a fruit vendor's stand and harass an elegantly dressed woman on the New York wharves in this 1857 oil painting entitled After a Long Cruise. Sodden sailors themselves were often victimized by unscrupulous owners of saloons and boardinghouses. "They worked like horses at sea," observed one clipper captain, "and spent their money like asses ashore."*

criteria as the creak of the ship's mast butts, the rhythm of her timbers and the rush of water past her hull.

Running the ship at the very limit of her potential sometimes unnerved the other officers. A passenger who sailed aboard the *Nightingale* from New York to Melbourne in 1854 recalled an occasion when a first mate named Bartlett came on duty at 4 p.m. and found the maintopgallant sail straining in a heavy blow. "Captain Mather," the mate said tentatively to his commander, "that maintopgallant sail is laboring very hard." He suggested that the sail should be reefed. "It is drawing well," replied the captain; "let it stand, Mr. Bartlett."

Two hours later, when Bartlett was relieved by the second mate, the captain still stood at the weather rail, and as Bartlett went below he heard his replacement repeat his own anxious concern: "Captain Mather, that maintopgallant sail is struggling hard." Replied the captain implacably, "It holds a good full. Let it stand, Mr. Macfarland."

A similar recollection of a captain's determination survives in the journal of a passenger aboard Donald McKay's crack clipper *Lightning* on her way to Melbourne: "Top gallant sails not taken in although the blocks 18 inches above the lee rail are frequently under water—the deck is on an angle of 45° to 50°," he recorded in awe. "The second mate, whose watch it is, says, 'Now this is what I call carrying on!' "

So volatile was the combination of a resentful crew and the need for an all-out, life-imperiling performance that every clipper captain believed in iron discipline. The captain who became most famous—indeed, infamous—for this belief was Robert Waterman, and the engine of his notoriety was the *Challenge's* maiden voyage.

Waterman must have been in a particularly foul mood the day the *Challenge* left New York. Besides injuring the steward, he almost immediately fell into an argument with his first mate and fired him on the spot.

He now faced a choice of promoting his second mate, a shifty-looking fellow of uncertain talents named Alexander Coghill, or finding someone else. The decision was made easy for him. It happened that the well-known packet ship *Guy Mannering* sat at anchor near Sandy Hook, awaiting a favorable tide for her entrance into New York Harbor. Just as Waterman was pondering how to replace his mate, a ship's boat put out from the *Mannering* and approached the *Challenge*. In the stern sat a hulking 200-pound figure whom Waterman recognized. He was James Douglass, first mate of the *Mannering* and known to Waterman by reputation as a "bucko" mate, the savage sort that crewmen hated. "Black" Douglass, as he was called by many an unhappy crew, was harsher than most. It was said of him that he "would rather have a knockdown fight with a lot of sailors than eat a good dinner."

The *Mannering's* boat came alongside, and Douglass climbed up the *Challenge's* rope ladder. Professing to have no desire to go ashore when the *Mannering* docked, Douglass asked if he could ship out aboard the *Challenge*. If Waterman had any scruples against bucko mates, he chose to ignore them now. He signed Douglass on immediately and ordered him to make the *Challenge* ready for sea without delay.

As the *Challenge* headed out into the open Atlantic, Waterman took a good look at the crew, and his mood darkened. Though he was responsible for the largest and most heavily sparred merchant ship on the seas, and a $60,000 cargo ranging from barrels of champagne to plates of boiler iron, he had only a handful of competent crewmen. Of the 56 men aboard, only six had ever taken a helm, and of those only three could make the splices, sailor's knots and general rigging repairs that qualified them as able-bodied seamen. One half of the crew had never sailed before, and several had clearly come aboard for no better reason than to get a free ride to California and its gold. Some had just been released from New York jails. Many were Dutch, French, Italian or German; some spoke little or no English, and thus would barely be able to understand commands. Waterman knew better than to expect a high-quality crew from crimps—the source of most of this lot. But it seemed to Waterman that his pickings were worse than usual, probably because hundreds of other vessels had sailed from New York in the last few months, and the waterfront had been stripped of seamen.

After huddling with his officers, Waterman called all hands aft and gave them a stern lecture. They were crew members of the clipper ship *Challenge* whether they liked it or not, and whether they liked it or not they were going to learn to become sailors. If they obeyed orders, they would be treated fairly; one sign of insubordination or even malinger-

This 19th Century sailor's bludgeon
of braided leather, its weighted ends neatly
worked in cord hitching, illustrates how
nautical arts were put to violent uses.
When wary captains confiscated pistols
and knives, their men often crafted arsenals
of such makeshift but effective weapons.

ing, and they would suffer for it. As he harangued the crew, studying their resentful faces, he stretched out his threats to provide time for the mates to complete a mission he had given them. Methodically they went through every sea chest and duffel bag in the forecastle, collecting a formidable arsenal of pistols, bowie knives, slingshots and knuckledusters, which they took on deck and tossed into the sea. Waterman then ordered the crewmen to form a line and file past the ship's carpenter, who stood at an anvil and knocked off the tip of the sailor's knife that every man carried in his belt. Waterman could not have these knives thrown overboard; a sailor would be helpless aloft without a knife to cut open stubborn knots. But without tips the knives would be less dangerous weapons in case of trouble.

This somber ceremony was followed by a labor-apportioning ritual standard to all ships at the start of a voyage. In these few minutes the demanding regimen of the months ahead was immutably fixed by the first and second mates, who divided the men into two watches and made the work assignments. About half a dozen crewmen—the carpenter, the cook, the sailmaker and other specialists—were exempt from the watches; they worked whatever hours their special functions called for. From the remaining hands assembled before them, the first and second mates took turns choosing. The first mate selected the man he deemed the likeliest-looking candidate and ordered him to step to the port side of the ship; the second mate then chose a man and directed him to the starboard side. Both mates continued in this manner until the division was complete. The so-called port and starboard watches each served four hours on duty, followed by four hours off—but the off-duty hours were not necessarily free time; the men could be turned out for special tasks whenever an officer wished. The period between 4 p.m. and 8 p.m. was broken into two two-hour shifts. This alternated the schedule day by day so that one group of men did not always have to take the unpopular midnight to 4 a.m. watch.

The men were put to work at once. Some were ordered to heave at the standing rigging—the stays and shrouds that held the masts in place—tightening loose lines and taking the strain off excessively taut ones. Other men were sent into the running rigging aloft to work the sails. They climbed up the ratlines, then out to the ends of the yards, getting such purchase as they could on the thin footropes under their heels. Then, no matter how the spars might swing if the wind was blowing hard, no matter how stiff and heavy a rain-drenched sail might be, they had to grasp the canvas and either reef it or shake it out, according to the captain's orders.

No one, not even the greenest or youngest hand, had any grace period to postpone the fearful experience of climbing the towering masts; all hands were sent aloft early in their first watch. But a wise mate would mix his new hands with whatever veterans he had aboard; these men, once they had sobered up and regained their sea legs, knew their way out onto the footropes. Following their example, the newcomers learned to climb the weather side of the rigging—the side from which the wind was blowing—to take advantage of the angle at which the ship was heeled. They also learned to keep their eyes fastened on their work. Any

# Essential tools for the master of many trades

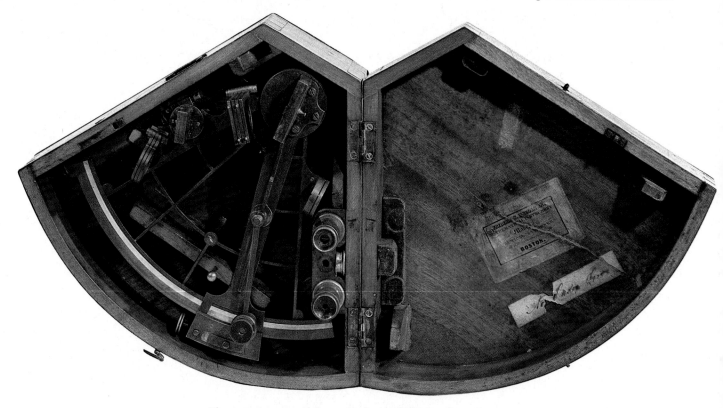

*This brass and wood telescope—known as a glass—belonged to Captain John Nickerson of the North America.*

The men who captained clipper ships had to be much more than expert sailors and strong-willed commanders. A clipper captain was a Jack-of-all-trades, usually serving as the ship's chief navigator, meteorologist, signalman and, when the necessity arose, its doctor.

To perform these diverse tasks, a captain required a variety of tools, many of them personal possessions that he toted from clipper to clipper. They included navigational aids such as Matthew Fontaine Maury's revolutionary *Wind and Current Charts* and *Sailing Directions*, tide tables and a nautical almanac containing detailed astronomical tables. These guides were used in conjunction with an array of navigational instruments, most prominently a compass, a sextant and a chronometer, whose accuracy permitted longitude to be computed to within a fraction of a degree.

In his role as weatherman, any prudent captain took along his own barometer. Failure to do so could be disastrous: In 1857 the captain of the American clipper *Mississippi* set sail without his barometer and was caught unawares by a hurricane in the Atlantic. The *Mississippi* lost all of her masts and, leaking badly, limped into a British port three weeks late.

Hardly less critical among the captain's paraphernalia was his medicine chest. With the help of tonics, medical instruments and a copy of Dr. Abraham T. Lowe's *Sailor's Guide to Health*, the captain treated the crew for everything from boils or broken legs to the injuries sailors sometimes inflicted on one another during melees in the forecastle.

*The sextant measured the angle of celestial bodies above the horizon. After making sextant sightings and noting the time, the captain used his nautical almanac to calculate his position.*

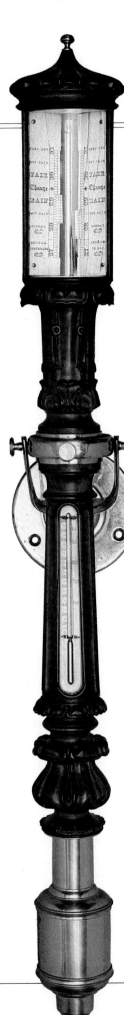

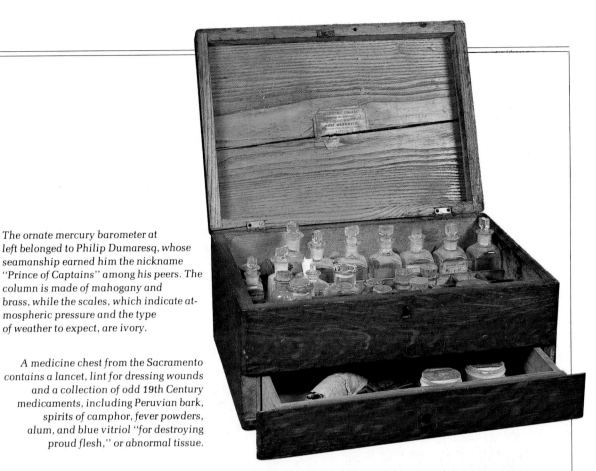

The ornate mercury barometer at
left belonged to Philip Dumaresq, whose
seamanship earned him the nickname
"Prince of Captains" among his peers. The
column is made of mahogany and
brass, while the scales, which indicate at-
mospheric pressure and the type
of weather to expect, are ivory.

A medicine chest from the Sacramento
contains a lancet, lint for dressing wounds
and a collection of odd 19th Century
medicaments, including Peruvian bark,
spirits of camphor, fever powders,
alum, and blue vitriol "for destroying
proud flesh," or abnormal tissue.

Signal flags like these enabled a captain to communicate
with foreign skippers and port authorities without knowing their
languages. The flags were read by using an international code.

neophyte who made the mistake of looking down through the long network of rigging was likely to panic and freeze—but if he did so he would be startled out of his paralysis by an ear-blistering oath from the mate.

Partly through fear of punishment, partly through the instinct for self-preservation, the novices soon learned how to keep their balance. The alternative was to plunge into the seas below or, worse, onto the deck, which could break a man's back or smash his head like a melon. Practice helped in these aerial labors, and the new sailors soon discovered that they would get plenty of that. It seemed that no sooner had they regained the deck after reefing sail than they were sent aloft to let it out again because the wind had moderated fractionally.

Less terrifying, but infinitely tedious, was the work of holystoning the deck—rubbing the planks clean with a prayer book-sized chunk of sandstone. At any hour of the day or night, any crewmen who were not needed in the rigging might be ordered down on their knees to carry out that job. Some captains and mates made their watches holystone even under the light of the moon, and the man who dallied over the task was as subject to the mate's lash as one who dawdled in the rigging.

The men aboard the *Challenge* were more stubborn than most about settling into the ship's routine—or so it seemed to Captain Waterman. "They would fight among themselves, cut, gouge, bite and kept in a continual row," he later recalled. The only way they could be held to their work was by constant haranguing and lashing—treatment that First Mate Douglass seemed only too eager to dispense. Sometimes he beat them with billets of wood or his knotty fists, and it became clear that when his blood was up he could barely control himself. Before the ship was many days out, the passengers noted that crewmen were gathering in groups and muttering about the treatment meted out on board.

The resentment of the crew exploded into violence one month out of New York. One Sunday morning, when the *Challenge* was off Rio de Janeiro, moving along well before a moderate southeast trade wind, several hands reported to Douglass that they were missing some of their belongings. Douglass ordered every man on deck with his sea chest, to see if the missing items could be found. While he stood over them and speeded the proceedings with his menacing belaying pin, each man was made to empty his sea chest in front of the others.

It was nearly noon, and Waterman had just come onto the poop deck with his sextant to take the noon sighting. As he went to the weather rail and aimed his sextant at the horizon, he was startled to hear from the foredeck a sudden cry of "Murder!"

It was Douglass' voice. Waterman put down his sextant, ran to the edge of the quarter-deck and saw that some 20 men were assaulting Douglass. One had grabbed the mate from behind by the throat and thrown him to the deck. More than a dozen others leaped into the attack, flashing sailor's knives.

Waterman picked up an iron belaying pin, jumped down the quarter-deck steps and raced forward toward Douglass, who was roaring curses and lurching like a wounded bear in his efforts to shake off his attackers. Waterman waded in with the belaying pin, swinging it with both hands and knocking down three men. Seizing one of the attackers, Waterman

*Roused by the cry, "All hands reef tops'ils," crewmen tumble from their fo'c's'le berths and sprint for the deck in this sketch from the 1863 journal of a Sumatra-bound sailor. Seafaring skill was critical at the sudden onset of a squall, for a laggard crew could find the ship riding with tattered sails, or even dismasted, in a matter of minutes.*

wrenched him away, marched him across the deck and tied him to the rigging. Douglass helped him subdue and tie up another half-dozen crewmen. The rest of the men lost heart and fled to the forecastle.

By the time the melee had ended, Douglass had 12 knife wounds. He staggered aft on Waterman's arm. While the captain tended the wounds, Douglass reported that the first man to jump him and stab him had been a seaman named Fred Birkenshaw, who belonged to the starboard watch.

Just then the second mate, supervisor of that watch, came up from below to see what the commotion was about. "Mr. Coghill," said Douglass, "I want you to look for that man and be damned quick about it."

"What man?" asked the second mate.

"That man Fred, in your watch," Douglass shouted.

Coghill took a lantern and went into the gloomy forecastle. He was gone for some time before he returned to report that he could not locate Birkenshaw; in the confusion that followed Waterman's appearance on deck, Birkenshaw had last been seen slipping behind the pigpen forward of the mainmast.

"God damn their souls," Douglass exclaimed; "I'm glad the row has occurred. I can lick them as much as I like and they can't do anything with me when I get to California." Before this incident, Douglass' bucko ways could conceivably have been censured, in the unlikely event that he was called to account for them; but assaulting a mate could be interpreted as mutiny. Now, he reasoned, he would be justified in the eyes of the owners and of the law for any measures he might choose to take to keep the men in hand.

Waterman took steps to find out whether the incident had been a spur-of-the-moment uprising or a plot. He invited the four passengers to his cabin and then, before these witnesses, interrogated the crewmen one by one. As W. C. Marston, one of the passengers, later remembered the scene, the first crewman to appear, a fellow named George Smith, denied knowing anything at all about the disturbance. Waterman threatened him with a flogging for withholding information, and Smith changed his story. Yes, he said at last, a mutiny had been planned; a plot had been brewing for some time to overpower both Douglass and Waterman. The attempt had been set for the previous night, but had not come off because neither the mate nor the captain had been on deck at the right time.

The next two men to be interrogated confirmed Smith's account, and Waterman bullied them into revealing the names of eight conspirators. One was Birkenshaw, who was still nowhere to be found and was presumed by some to have jumped overboard. The others were swiftly apprehended. Calling all hands aft for an object lesson, Waterman had the alleged mutineers stripped to the waist, tied by their wrists to the rigging and then flogged. At length, the accused men were carried moaning and bleeding to their bunks, and the rest of the crew dispersed in a mood of profound dejection under the malevolent scowls of the captain and his first mate.

The thoughts of Captain Waterman during these days are difficult to divine, and he left no record to throw light on the matter. Presumably he had fears for his personal safety; passengers later testified that he began keeping a pistol at his side, as did Douglass. Presumably, too, Water-

*This satirical version of a Christmas Day menu, created by an American sailor in 1859, offers such delicacies as "rats smothered in oil" and "cockroaches on half shell." But to many seamen, an even worse trial than dreary meals was the banning of liquor on American clippers, enforced because insurance firms gave discounts for "voyages performed without consumption of spirits."*

# The age-old reign of the lash

"The right to flog," declared author James Fenimore Cooper in an 1844 treatise on corporal punishment at sea, is "not in harmony with the spirit of the age." The age's enlightened spirit notwithstanding, the ancient practice of maintaining discipline by the lash was still very much a part of shipboard life in the mid-19th Century—particularly on clippers, whose masters believed that only the sternest measures could ensure the crew performance necessary to keep their complex sailing machines moving at top speed.

Flogging was a grimly efficient ritual. The unfortunate sailor was first stripped to the waist and then bound to the rigging or a grating on the main deck, hands tied above his head, legs spread apart and ankles tied. Usually the boatswain's mate wielded the cat-o'-nine-tails, an ugly instrument made of a wooden handle and nine braided or twisted hemp cords, each 18 inches long and knotted near the end.

The entire crew had to watch the beating, its purpose being as much to cow the other sailors into unquestioning obedience as to punish the malefactor. Few witnesses forgot the experience. Recalled one seaman, "Still the dull whacks resound in my ears, followed by a low moan when the boatswain's mate stopped and the poor fellow was taken down, his shirt flung over his bleeding back."

The most trivial offense could call down an unmerciful whipping. United States Navy records of shipboard punishment meted out during the late 1840s mention penalties of six lashes for "slow motion in getting into a boat," 12 for "stealing poultry from the coop" and 12 for "dirty and unwashed clothes." Clipper crews received even harsher sentences, totally at the master's discretion: A man who so much as hesitated before replying to his captain's question could be flogged senseless. And clipper seamen usually had no recourse to a ship's surgeon, who often intervened on a Naval vessel to reduce the number of lashes imposed.

Harrowing descriptions that were published by Cooper and other authors—most notably Richard Henry Dana, whose book *Two Years before the Mast* stirred a fierce debate on the mistreatment of sailors—prodded Congress into forbidding flogging on all American ships in 1850. Captains of clipper ships, however, generally ignored the law and continued to flog into the 1860s, giving their crews the dubious distinction of being among the last American seamen to suffer under the lash. British clipper sailors fared even worse; flogging was not outlawed on their ships until 1879.

*American seamen, complying with the order "All hands on deck to witness punishment," watch a shipmate's ordeal.*

man had legitimate worries for the safety of his vessel and the cargo she carried. Whatever the case, he became increasingly harsh as the voyage proceeded, and he condoned, if he did not initiate, behavior on the part of his first mate that exceeded the demands of discipline and brought on new crises.

One day during a gale in the roaring forties, Waterman assembled all hands on deck and ordered a reef in the mizzen topsail. Second Mate Coghill led his watch up the ratlines and out onto the pitching yard to do the job. It was perilous and frightening work; the ship was rolling from side to side in the mountainous seas, nearly dipping the tips of the mizzen-topsail yard into the water, and the rigging was snapping back and forth in the powerful gusts. The hands of the crewmen were so numb from the cold that they could scarcely get a grip on the drenched and stubborn canvas.

To Douglass, whose men on the deck were responsible for working the lines to loosen the sail, it seemed that Coghill and his team were too slow about their job. He bellowed at Coghill to move the men faster, threatening to come up and kick them himself if need be. As the *Challenge* pitched and yawed, one of Coghill's men suddenly lost his grip, fell backward and plunged screaming into the sea.

Without seeming to give a moment's thought to saving the fallen man, the two mates exchanged accusations of incompetence. Coghill shouted that everyone on the yard would go if Douglass did not trim the upper yard—shift its angle to spill the wind from the sail. The men on deck obliged, but an edge of the sail whipped loose and flapped up over the yard with such force that two more men lost their purchase and plummeted like cannon balls into the hissing water. Another seaman, later reconstructing the incident, recalled that Coghill himself had kicked them, in spiteful reaction to Douglass' nagging. However that may be, Coghill prodded his remaining men to grab at the flailing canvas and get on with their task of bunching it into rolls along the yard. By the time the job was done and the men were allowed to descend the ratlines to the deck, they were trembling from exhaustion and terror.

Death aboard ship was common enough; even a well-run vessel might lose two or three men in a stiff blow, and old hands would take it in stride. In such a sea as this there was no hope of rescuing the lost men; they could not have lived more than a minute or two in the near-freezing water. Nonetheless, the two mates' dogged attention to their personal quarrel, without so much as acknowledging the loss of three men's lives, was a spectacle that served only to intensify the bitterness of the hands toward their officers. Some took sick and did not appear on deck for the next watch.

From the outset of the voyage, so many of the crew had been ill that Waterman had had the sail room converted into a sick bay. A number of the men had come on board already suffering from dysentery, jaundice, tuberculosis, delirium tremens, syphilis and gonorrhea. Others, who had been dumped on the ship with no clothing except the shirts and trousers they were wearing, came down with chilblains and frostbite as the clipper neared the antarctic latitudes, then in the grip of the Southern Hemisphere's winter. But after the night the three men fell from the rigging, a dozen or more of the crew began pleading illness most of the time. Although the condition of a few men was undeniably serious (four lives would be claimed by various diseases before the voyage was over), Waterman concluded that many, if not most, were malingering.

Among the crewmen was a Finn, variously called Tons Miti and Ions Smiti. One day when Smiti was holystoning the deck, Waterman beat him for working too slowly. Smiti, who could not speak a word of English, tried to explain with sign language that his legs were burning with chilblains and that he could hardly walk. The plea did nothing to soften the heart of the captain, although on the next occasion he suspected Smiti of malingering he vented his wrath more indirectly. "I ordered the mate to give him the rope's end, and I think he deserved it," Waterman recalled; "he appeared to walk well enough when going to the galley for his tea."

On another day a foremast hand named George Lessig—a scraggly-bearded complainer called "the Dancing Master" by his shipmates because he was so nimble at dodging the rope—refused to go aloft when ordered to reef sails. He protested that he had dysentery. "Go aft, then!" thundered Douglass in a rage. "The captain will cure you."

Waterman responded with a unique form of cure. "I think we will baptize you," he snarled. He signaled to Douglass, directing the mate's attention to the lee scuppers—the channels that drained away water from the deck. A heavy wave had just swept over the bow, and the waterway was awash with frigid, frothy sea water. The mate, reading the captain's intention at once, ran aft, seized Lessig and tossed him into the gurgling scuppers. When Lessig jumped up spouting, Douglass leaped onto him and forced him under again. Then the mate pulled the drenched Lessig from the waterway and dragged him across the deck to the weather side and tied him to the rail. For several hours, Lessig huddled there, shivering in his wet shirt and trousers as the wind whipped about his body, until Douglass finally freed him and allowed him to slink back to his bunk.

Lessig did not appear on deck the next morning, nor indeed did he report for the next 10 days. Finally a passenger, whose curiosity led him to the forecastle, found the seaman in his bunk—clearly suffering, as he had said, from dysentery. The passenger, possessed of more pity than common sense, gave him a massive dose of castor oil. Lessig died a few days afterward.

As the voyage progressed, Douglass seemed to advance from mere sadism to near derangement. When he got into a tiff with a hand called Papaw, he lost his head. Papaw was a grizzled Italian who spoke no English. He was also shoeless, and was afflicted with frostbite. One day, after the captain had beaten him for being too slow at his work, the old man did not come out on deck. Douglass had him dragged from the forecastle and brought to him for questioning. But Papaw could not understand what the mate was saying, nor could he answer in English anyway. Douglass beat him with his fists until the old man broke away and ran back to the forecastle.

Douglass followed the Italian to his bunk, pulled him out of it and then resumed pummeling the man's face and ribs. When his violence was spent, he let Papaw drop in a quivering heap and stomped back to the deck. A seaman named Charles Weldon, who carried the old man back to his bunk, remembered that his face was a pulp, his eyes were swollen and sightless, his head was blood-smeared and his hair was matted. According to the recollection of another sailor, Waterman—perhaps stricken with remorse—visited the old man in his bunk, bringing him wine and water to drink. But he was too late to be of help. An hour later Papaw was dead.

During these nightmarish days, Birkenshaw, who was the suspected ringleader of the mutiny, was nowhere to be seen. Some of the crew suggested to the officers that he had jumped overboard when Waterman waded into the melee. But Douglass, realizing that few men would plunge to certain death in the desolation of the South Atlantic, felt sure that Birkenshaw was hiding somewhere in the ship, and he was determined to find him. The most likely refuge was the forecastle, but no sooner had the mate crossed its threshold in search of the offender than someone blew out the lantern. In the darkness Douglass could sense the men's hostility toward him and, rather than proceed far enough to let himself be surrounded, he retreated. A few days later he made a second attempt—with the same result.

He gave up these forays but continually badgered the hands on deck for information. Eventually he learned that Birkenshaw was just where he had suspected. Fearing now to go into the forecastle himself, Douglass sent a teen-age cabin boy to persuade the culprit to come out. The boy had to crawl under the farthest forward bunk into a dark cubicle that was normally occupied by nothing but spare lines. He touched something warm, cried out and scurried back on deck. On his heels came the bearded and emaciated fugitive.

Since stabbing Douglass, Birkenshaw had spent a month in that black hole, feeding on handouts brought by friends. But he had finally had enough and, knowing that Douglass had discovered his whereabouts anyway, had come out to face his fate. "I will make a full confession," he said as he approached Douglass. "Don't hurt me."

Douglass, never a forgiving man, was in no mood to be lenient now. "I've got the son of a bitch!" he shouted out to Waterman, who was pacing by the weather rail of the quarter-deck. At this, Waterman exploded: "Down on your knees, you son of a bitch. What did you intend doing with me?" Birkenshaw quickly lost his resolve to confess; instead, he replied that he had had nothing to do with the mutiny. To Waterman, who had wrestled the man off Douglass' back at the time of the attack, such an answer was intolerable. Raising the club that he carried, he swung at Birkenshaw. The mutineer lifted his arm to ward off the blow, and his arm broke as the club hit.

Birkenshaw was consigned to join the rest of the men in sick bay, where his broken arm was left shackled and untended as the *Challenge* made her unhappy way to San Francisco. From then on, Waterman and Douglass often had to work the ship almost alone; some days they found only three out of 27 men turning up for a watch. The second mate was frequently among the missing.

The *Challenge* reached San Francisco in 108 days. The voyage had taken 18 days longer than the Griswolds had stipulated, so Waterman lost his $10,000 bonus. But much worse troubles for him lay ahead.

After he had brought the *Challenge* up to her pilot off the Farallon Islands on the morning of October 28, and come in through the Golden Gate to anchor off Alcatraz Island, he signaled for a Coast Guard cutter and turned over the eight men he believed to have been the ringleaders of the mutiny. Then he summoned the rest of the crew aft and announced that he intended to have the others involved arrested for mutiny. He must have known he was only making an idle threat; within hours the *Challenge* was surrounded at her anchorage by boatloads of crimps, who swiftly made off with nearly every crewman not confined to sick bay.

Waterman and his first mate had no such freedom to leave the ship because both were personally responsible for the cargo. The port was so crowded that two days passed before the *Challenge* could tie up at the Pacific Street wharf and engage stevedores to unload her. During those two days, while Waterman, Douglass, and the sick remained aboard, the men who had gone off with the crimps spread tales of their hellish voyage through every saloon and waterfront boardinghouse in San Fran-

cisco. By the time Waterman had disembarked on October 30, he found a number of boats gathered around the *Challenge*, every one filled with glowering seamen. The dock was equally crowded, and as Waterman came ashore he had to force his way through a milling mob of angry men.

Waterman got through, but Douglass, whose reputation for malice long antedated this voyage of the *Challenge*, decided he had better not step into the crowd on the pier. He waited until the mob was distracted by the hustling of the stevedores. Then he caught the attention of Commodore T. H. Allen, overseer of the dock workers hired by the *Challenge*'s owners. Allen rowed a boat around to the far side of the vessel. Douglass climbed down the rope ladder into it, and Allen bent to the oars. They had no sooner rounded the *Challenge*'s stern than they were spied by the besieging boatmen. The only escape route was through an anchored fleet of ships that had been abandoned by their gold-hungry crews. Allen raced in that direction, and an eerie chase ensued.

The anchorage was a maze of ghostly hulls that creaked as they rode at their moorings. The thump of the oarlocks and drip of the oars echoed and reechoed as Allen and Douglass slid swiftly between the high walls of decaying wood and rusting iron. Behind them they could hear their

*Ships abandoned in favor of the gold fields form a waterborne ghost town in San Francisco harbor in this 1853 daguerreotype. Seamen infected with gold fever sometimes jumped ship even before anchoring. Some of the ships at right are working vessels that have managed to retain their crews.*

pursuers baying to one another down the long corridors of the lifeless fleet. Emerging from the maze, Allen put his back into it, and the boat shot across the open water and slithered onto the beach at Rincon Point, a relatively undeveloped area south of the Embarcadero. Douglass jumped ashore and ran for the underbrush. A howling pack of boatmen landed and fanned out after him. They soon were back on the beach. With a speed and cunning born of desperation, Douglass had got away.

Two days later the *California Courier* printed a story that carried the tale beyond the waterfront, arousing the passions of all San Franciscans. "The ship *Challenge* has arrived," it said, "and Captain Waterman, her commander, has also—but where are nine of her crew? And where is he and his guilty mate? The accounts given of Captain Waterman towards his men, if true, make him one of the most inhuman monsters of this age. If they are true, he should be burned alive."

The newspaper's words were tantamount to a call for a lynching party, and before the day had ended a crowd of some 2,000 discontented seamen and other waterfront hangers-on had assembled at the pier—in time to see the remaining half-dozen sick and injured men moved from the *Challenge* on stretchers bound for the Marine Hospital in San Francisco. Most of the invalids were probably suffering from dysentery and scurvy that they had had before coming aboard in New York, or that they might have contracted aboard any ship in 1851. But to the mob they looked like nothing so much as proof of cruelty on the part of Waterman and Douglass. Someone struck up a cry for Waterman, and soon the whole mob was advancing toward California Street and the Alsop Building, local headquarters of the Griswold agents.

Charles Griswold, who was representing his family's firm in San Francisco, met the mob at the door. The crowd shouted for Waterman. Griswold replied that he was not there. The mob surged back and forth, and someone suggested rushing the door. To forestall violence, Griswold invited a committee of six men to search the building. After much shouting and wrangling, a delegation was selected.

Griswold's delaying tactic had given Waterman time to climb to the roof and make his escape through the building next door. But inside the Griswold office the mob's committee found another captain, John Land, who was scheduled to take the *Challenge* on the next leg of her voyage, to China. To the astonishment of Captain Land, a white-haired and mild-mannered man, the delegation seized him and dragged him outdoors. Surrender Bully Waterman, someone shouted, or they would hang Captain Land—and the crowd took up the cry.

The tumult was suddenly silenced by the pealing of the Monumental Engine Company's fire bell. In the absence of an actual fire, the engine company's bell was the rallying signal for the San Francisco Vigilance Committee—a group of 600-odd self-appointed keepers of the peace who, off and on for almost a year, had been dealing out eye-for-an-eye justice without going through due process of law. Recently the vigilantes, many of whom were acquiring new-found decorum with their burgeoning wealth, had been quiescent. In the present instance, they had remained aloof from the rabble at the wharf. But now, with dire trouble threatening at the waterfront, they offered their services to the mayor.

## Brave women afloat in a man's world

*Mary Wakeman made three round trips between New York and San Francisco with her captain-husband, Edgar.*

The shy, pretty young woman clinging to her husband's arm in the picture above hardly seems suited to the brutal life aboard a clipper, yet she spent four years with her skipper-husband on the *Adelaide*. During that time, the first mate killed a seaman by knocking him overboard, another sailor murdered the mate, and the murderer was in turn hanged from a yardarm. Mary Wakeman took all these events with fortitude; she also bore two children at sea, with only her husband to act as midwife (the first was christened Adelaide Seaborn Wakeman).

Mary Wakeman was not the only woman who found that sailing with a clipper-captain spouse entailed rigors and dangers she never knew ashore. Sally Low, 19 years old, was spending her honeymoon aboard the *N. B. Palmer* in 1852 when a mutinous seaman shot the first mate in the leg; her husband, Captain Charles Low, subdued and later flogged the offender. The wife of clipper master Thomas Andrews—her first name did not survive in the records—scarcely slept during a 29-day Cape Horn gale that smashed the spars of the *Red Gauntlet* in 1856. She brewed tea for the crew and nursed the injured, winning the loyalty of the most callous seamen.

A woman aboard usually introduced a measure of compassion, and often engendered gratitude from the men. But no other clipper wife was more beloved, or more courageous, than Mary Ann Patten, who sailed from New York in 1856 with her husband, Joshua, commander of the *Neptune's Car*. As the ship reached the Strait of Le Maire, east of Cape Horn, Captain Patten was stricken by "a brain fever," losing his sight and falling into delirium. Mary, who had just learned she was pregnant, took command of the ship.

She had taught herself navigation on an earlier voyage to Hong Kong, and the crew now depended on her to reckon the vessel's position. As she guided the clipper through one of the worst storms ever recorded off Cape Horn, the sailors followed her orders without hesitation. "Each man," reported one observer, "vied with his fellows in the performance of his duty."

For 50 days she nursed her husband—studying medical texts when she could snatch a moment—and continued to command the ship, sleeping in her clothes in order to be ready for any emergency on deck. She brought the *Neptune's Car* into San Francisco on November 15, 1856. "Few persons would imagine," wrote one journalist, "that the woman who behaved so bravely is a slender New England girl, scarcely twenty years old."

Four months later Mary Patten gave birth to a son, and four months after that her husband, who probably had advanced tuberculosis, died. Newspapers as far away as London had extolled her heroism, but she dismissed all accolades. When the insurers of the *Neptune's Car* sent her a $1,000 reward for saving the vessel, she wrote back, "I fear you have overestimated those services. Without the hearty cooperation of the crew, the ship could not have arrived safely."

The mayor, with few police at his disposal, could not control a disturbance of this size without them.

Now, upon the clangorous tolling of the fire bell, the vigilantes came swarming into California Street and took up positions around the mob. Although outnumbered by more than 3 to 1, the vigilantes were armed, and their guns made an impressive showing against the outraged but largely weaponless mob. Within a few minutes the throng had obeyed the mayor's order to disperse, and Captain John Land walked back into the Alsop Building.

By this time the law had caught up with Douglass. The morning after his escape into the scrub of Rincon Point, three men had found him in a cart 10 miles outside of San Francisco, sleeping off a drunk: He was on the San Jose road, bound for Monterey and a steamer to Panama. Too dazed to resist capture when the sheriff and a posse arrived, Douglass announced with boozy bravado, "I whipped 'em and I'll whip 'em again." As he started back to the city at the end of a rope wound around his arms and shoulders, he bowed with mock courtesy and said, "Well, gentlemen, if you want to hang me, here's a pretty tree. Do it like men." Sheriff Jack Hays preferred the more legal route, but evidently was sympathetic to the condemned man's other requests: The trip back to San Francisco took all morning because, Hays explained, "the prisoner insisted on taking a drink at every bar along the road." When at last the party reached San Francisco toward noon on November 1, the sheriff threw the mate into jail to await trial on charges of murder and assault brought by the federal government.

Robert Waterman, meanwhile, remained in hiding until November 11, when he emerged voluntarily and demanded court action against Birkenshaw and his accomplices. For the next two months San Francisco's United States District Court rocked with sensational charges and countercharges that exposed the seamier side of clipper-ship sailing. About half a dozen trials followed one after another, but the records of the cases are sketchy, and the details—even some of the results—have been lost. Certainly Waterman and Douglass accused Birkenshaw and the others of mutiny; Birkenshaw and his former comrades in turn accused the captain and his first mate of murder and assault.

The juries faced a difficult task, and their job was not made any easier by the fact that tales from the *Challenge* had been many times magnified as they spread through San Francisco bars and were trumpeted in newspapers. According to one story, Waterman had struck down a helmsman for having dirty hands; according to another, he was guilty of shooting the three men who had fallen from the rigging. In still another tale, an injured sailor was supposed to have been sewed up in a tarpaulin and pushed overboard, still groaning as he went over the rail.

As the trials progressed, there seemed no doubt that Waterman and Douglass had been excessive in their harshness. One foremast hand testified that, even before the attack on Douglass, the men were beaten nearly every day with belaying pins, sticks and clubs, heavers and ropes. Another sailor concurred: "I was beat with a club myself. I did not disobey orders; the first intimation I had was a crack on the head."

Neither did there seem any doubt that the seamen themselves left much to be desired. "It was the worst crew I've ever seen," said Waterman, adding: "I have been to sea for the last 30 years." Even some of the seamen endorsed that opinion. "We had a miserable crew on board the *Challenge*," testified one 40-year veteran; "most were miserable trash."

Birkenshaw was found not guilty. The other accused members of the crew were also set free (it is not clear from contemporary accounts whether they ever came to trial). James Douglass was convicted of cruelty to Smiti and of murdering Papaw, the Italian, but he served no sentence. There is no record of what penalty, if any, the court assessed in his case, but Douglass was shortly released. He did pay a penalty of a personal sort, however; he was never signed on by another shipper.

Waterman was found guilty of one charge—the beating of Ions Smiti—even though the court could not locate a speaker of Finnish to interpret Smiti's testimony; possibly the jury found the bruised seaman too pitiable to need words. Despite that guilty verdict, however, the judge handed down no sentence. The jury failed to reach a verdict on whether Waterman was guilty of beating Birkenshaw. The district attorney—perhaps because the passengers sided with Waterman, and perhaps because a crucial witness among the seamen could not be sobered up long enough to testify—entered a nolle prosequi, a notice that he would proceed no further with the other charges against the captain. Waterman went free.

Curiously, it was the *Challenge* that suffered most from the episode. Like every other ship, she had a personality and a reputation. She had earned a bad name on her maiden voyage, and she was fated to carry the stigma of being a hellship ever after. When Captain Land was making ready to take her on from San Francisco to Hong Kong, he was able to get a crew only after the Griswold company had paid a $200 advance to every seaman for signing on. And the *Challenge* suffered two more mutinies before she foundered and sank off the coast of France in 1876.

When the trials ended, Waterman made good on his resolve to retire. He sent for his wife and settled in California, where he took part in the founding of the town of Fairfield, about 40 miles from San Fransciso. He built a house with a prow like that of a ship, and devoted most of his time to raising prize poultry and cattle. But he kept an eye on maritime affairs; he served as Port Warden and Inspector of Hulls for San Francisco, and occasionally he lent a hand in salvaging shipwrecks on the shore of the Golden Gate. To Californians who knew him in his later years, when he had become a member of the established gentry, he seemed tough rather than cruel, and many of them had difficulty imagining that he could ever have personally beaten a seaman for failing to obey orders promptly. But then, they knew Bob Waterman only ashore, never as a clipper master confronted with an undisciplined crew at sea.

*The ill-fated clipper Challenge—her first captain having left the ship to stand trial for a murder that he allegedly committed between New York and San Francisco—sails into the harbor at Hong Kong, and into more misfortune, under her replacement skipper. In the crown colony the Royal Marines had to be summoned to discipline the Challenge's mutinous crew.*

# Chapter 4

# Every sea a racecourse, every voyage a trial of speed

In the fall of 1852 *Bell's Life*, a high-toned British sporting magazine, called attention to a notice that was appearing in the business pages of British daily newspapers. "The American Navigation Club," the notice said, "challenges the shipbuilders of Great Britain to a ship race, with cargo on board, from a port in England to a port in China and back." Specifying that the vessels were to be not less than 800 nor more than 1,200 tons—the size of contemporary clipper ships—the club proposed a bet of £10,000 on the contest. At the going rate of exchange, that worked out to about $50,000—roughly equivalent to the cost of building a clipper ship. To underscore the solemnity of the wager and the good faith of the bettors, the club members—a dozen or so Boston shipping merchants—engaged a prominent bank to act as guarantor and deposited the stake money in it for safekeeping. "The Americans want a match," *Bell's* editorialized in urging the contest upon its readers, "and it reflects somewhat upon our chivalry not to accommodate them."

The challenge had come in response to a number of boasts made by British shipbuilders and the British press during the previous year. Now that British shipbuilders had taken inspiration from the American vessel *Oriental* and launched two clippers of their own—the *Stornoway* in 1850 and the *Chrysolite* in 1851—they were growing disdainful of their American counterparts. "We, the British shipowners," said Richard Green of the famous Blackwall Line at a London banquet in 1851, "have at last sat down to play a fair and open game with the Americans, and by Jove, we'll trump them." When the *Chrysolite* logged the impressive time of 80 days on the London-Anyer Lor leg of her maiden voyage to China later that year, a British newspaper crowed: "The *Chrysolite* takes the palm." The Bostonians had heard enough, and now they were daring Britannia to put money behind her claim to rule the waves.

The bait was not taken. Perhaps the British saw no need to defend their prowess against the upstart Americans; more likely, they secretly thought they could not win, for despite all the boasting, neither the *Chrysolite* nor the *Stornoway* had yet matched the best American runs from China to London.

But in a real sense the race was on, and had been for three years, ever since the *Sea Witch* had inaugurated the reign of the clipper ship as queen of merchant vessels. And in the decade and a half that followed, clipper-ship racing continued to display all the excitement of a spectator sport. Clippers remained the major American and British carriers of express cargo—whether flour for California, mining tools for the Aus-

*Flying all sails with a breeze on the beam, the Ariel (foreground) and the Taeping slice through rolling seas as they run for London during the closest clipper contest ever, the Great Tea Race of 1866. Though the Ariel and the Taeping never drew quite this close, only about a mile separated them at the finish— an incredibly narrow margin after a 15,000-mile passage from China.*

tralia gold rush or tea for customers on both sides of the Atlantic—and more than 400 new ones were built. Every clipper carried with her on every voyage the hopes—and often the wagers—of builder and merchant, captain and crew, and countless fans among the public that she would outpace all her rivals.

As the 1850s wore on, a captain setting out from almost any port at more or less the same time as another captain heading the same way came to count it a matter of honor to bet a new beaver hat that his vessel would beat the other to their destination. His crewmen, meanwhile, were likely to be betting their counterparts a month's wages on the same proposition. And laymen who had no connection whatever with seafaring were also at it, wagering sums large and small and keeping abreast of the clippers' progress from one port to another as the news was flashed around the world by telegraph and reported in the newspapers.

Because clipper ships were so hard-driven and suffered a lot of wear in the first few years of their lives, most of them made their best runs on their first or second voyage. But, as Captain Robert Waterman's unhappy passage aboard the *Challenge* had shown in the summer and fall of 1851, newness was no guarantee of a glittering performance. In fact, the outcome of any clipper-ship race, whether with another vessel or against the record, hung on a combination of factors. Teamwork of the sort that had eluded Waterman and his crew was of paramount importance. So was a captain's familiarity with the route and his expertise in applying, in fair weather and foul, oceanographic and meteorological data. The reputation of the shipbuilder or of the ship herself also might make a difference; a well-touted vessel got preference among stevedores and pilots, and a ship thus favored might squeeze out a victory by leaving or arriving on an earlier tide than her rival, or even by having a more skillful pilot at the finish. And caprices of nature often played a critical role; an unexpected storm might bring a chance setback that would doom an otherwise favored ship.

Racing began informally enough. At first it was simply an individual matter of builders and captains trying to best the records of their colleagues. That competitive spirit—already apparent in 1851, when the *Flying Cloud* and the *Challenge* were among the 45 clipper ships that sailed for California from the East Coast, all of them trying to stay under the magic number of 100 days—swept the shipping industry the following year. In the 37-day period between October 11 and November 17 of 1852, no fewer than 15 clipper ships set out for San Francisco from New York and Boston, an average of one every three days. All their captains had the same objective in mind: to beat the 89-day record set by the *Flying Cloud* the year before.

The 1852 competition made history because three of the vessels involved, though they left New York on different days, were remarkably close to one another for much of the race. Right down to the home stretch, the glory of winning in elapsed time might have gone to any of the three. The captains glimpsed one another's ships often enough along the way to leave them in no doubt as to the closeness of the contest. Each ship, summed up Matthew Maury in a detailed report on the race in a

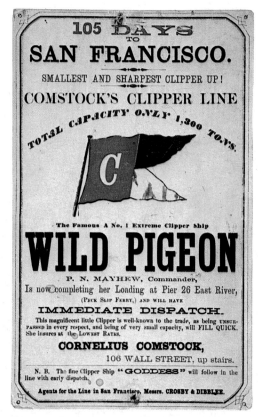

*Clipper owners advertised departures by handing out colorful four-by-six-inch sailing cards like these, trumpeting their vessels' virtues to shippers and prospective passengers. The cards shown here were printed several years after the Wild Pigeon, Flying Fish and John Gilpin had raced from New York to San Francisco in 1852. Two of the ships acquired new captains in the interim.*

subsequent edition of his *Wind and Current Charts*, "was driven at her topmost speed, the one almost in hail of the other, for three months, over a course of fifteen thousand miles in length."

The three clippers were well matched. One was the *Wild Pigeon*, a 996-ton, 189-foot vessel that on her maiden voyage the year before had made the run to San Francisco in a respectable 107 days. The second was the *Flying Fish*, also a year old and, at 1,505 tons and 207 feet in length, the largest; she had sped to San Francisco the previous year in 100 days and six hours. The third was the *John Gilpin*, 1,089 tons and 205 feet in length, and now on her maiden voyage.

All three were commanded by veteran captains: George Putnam on the *Wild Pigeon*, Justin Doane on the *John Gilpin*, and Edward Nickels on the *Flying Fish*. "Like steeds that know their riders," Maury said, "they were handled with the most exquisite skill and judgment, and in such hands they bounded out upon the glad waters most gracefully." Each captain, Maury proudly noted, had his *Wind and Current Charts* and *Sailing Directions*; each "had evidently studied them attentively, and each one was resolved to make the most of them, and do his best."

The *Wild Pigeon* was the first away, leaving New York on October 12, 1852. Seventeen days later the *John Gilpin* dropped her pilot and set forth, and three days after that the *Flying Fish* followed.

The *Wild Pigeon* ran into trouble almost at once. Captain Putnam noted in the ship's log that 13 days out of the first 19 were calm and stormy in alternation; the *Wild Pigeon* took 20 days just to reach the latitude of the West Indies.

Putnam had no sooner edged the *Pigeon* past the West Indies than conditions improved behind him. As a result, wrote Maury, "the *Gilpin* and the *Fish* came booming along, not under better management, indeed, but with a better run of luck and fairer courses before them." Both ships having embarked on the run down the North Atlantic just as the *Pigeon* completed it, they covered the same distance in 10 and eight days, respectively, rapidly gaining on the *Pigeon* (map, page 109). Despite her 17-day head start, the *Pigeon* crossed the Equator only seven days in the lead—which meant that she was now 10 days behind her rivals on elapsed time.

The *Flying Fish*, meanwhile, was running so well that she had caught the *John Gilpin*, and had left her three days astern. By November 17, only 16 days out of New York, she was 5° north of the Equator.

But now it was her turn for trouble. She was approaching Cape São Roque, Brazil, the headland that juts out into the Atlantic on the easternmost bulge of South America. Nickels had generally followed Maury's advice to go out to sea before heading south, in order to be in a position to steer a straight southerly course past the cape. But he had not gone out quite far enough, and now he was about 200 miles closer to the east coast of South America than Maury's charts deemed advisable. He would still have had no insurmountable problem if he had heeded Maury's next instruction, which was to "stand boldly on," meaning head due south through the doldrums; he could thus have made use of a land breeze off Brazil. But finding the *Flying Fish* slowed by the calms, Nickels "doubted the Charts," said Maury, "and committed *the* mistake of the passage."

Evidently thinking he would find better winds farther out to sea, Nickels turned eastward—the very direction he should not have taken. "The *Sailing Directions* had cautioned the navigator, again and again, not to attempt to fan along to the eastward in the equatorial doldrums," Maury lectured; by so doing the navigator would find himself engaged "in a fruitless strife with baffling airs, sometimes re-enforced in their weakness by westerly currents."

The move cost Nickels four days of the *Flying Fish's* valuable time. When at last he worked the ship out of the doldrums, he had made only 1° of southing. Maury, recounting the incident, pointed out that, while the *Flying Fish* was sloshing about in the doldrums, a slow merchantman had covered the same distance two days faster "by cutting straight across the doldrums, as the *Sailing Directions* advised him to do."

The other clipper ships, meanwhile, had followed Maury's charts to the letter, and had profited thereby. The *Pigeon* had made up a day of her earlier loss; she was now eight days in front and proceeding south along the coast of Brazil. The *Gilpin*, having crossed the doldrums and rounded Cape São Roque in seven days, had now come within 37 miles of the *Flying Fish*. But, of course, their captains were unaware of their relative standings in the race. Both ships were in the same latitude but were invisible over each other's horizon.

The next big challenge facing the three captains was the approach to Cape Horn, which thrusts a double barrier out into the Atlantic: Cape San Diego and Staten Island. The navigator has the choice of passing east around the far side of Staten Island or of cutting through the Strait of Le Maire, the body of water that runs between Cape San Diego and the island. The strait offers the shorter route, but it also presents greater navigational problems—strong currents, crosscurrents and tide rips so complex that Maury's charts had not yet accounted for all of them. The *Wild Pigeon*, 61 days out of New York on December 12, was the first to reach the area. With a good wind off the beam and all sails set, Putnam chose to take her into the Strait of Le Maire.

He chose wrong. No sooner was the *Pigeon* in the passage than the wind died. At the same time, Putnam found himself up against an unfavorable tide. Then, as he directed frantic sail adjustments to keep the *Pigeon* from drifting backward, he noticed something odd. There was another vessel in the strait—close enough for Putnam to make out her name, the *Realm*—and she was moving steadily ahead. Putnam deduced that her captain had found a current running in the opposite direction to the tide plaguing the *Pigeon*. His guess was supported by the fact that between the two vessels was "a race or tide rip that fairly roared and extended north and south as far as the eye could reach." Clearly, if he took the *Pigeon* into the path of the *Realm*, he could take advantage of the same current. But getting there presented a problem. The swirling waters, Putnam noted, "had the appearance of strong tide over rocks."

Putnam decided he had to take the risk. "I bore up and crossed," he later wrote. While everyone aboard the *Wild Pigeon* flinched and waited for the clipper to strike a reef, Putnam went on, "we were shaken violently, and whirled around in spite of helm and sails by rapid whirlpools."

But nothing worse was encountered, and slowly the clipper moved out of the maelstrom, whereupon "we had a change of tide, and we were soon up with the *Realm*."

However, the *Pigeon* was not past the strait's dangers yet. At about 10 o'clock the following night she was caught in a snow squall. "Lost no spars, but had some sails blow to pieces," Putnam recorded with skipperly understatement; in fact, he had nearly lost his top-hamper. The men worked doggedly to repair the damage, and the *Pigeon* pushed on. By December 14 she was clear of the strait, and at dawn on the following day, peering through a driving rain, Putnam could make out the soaring peak of Cape Horn. Then came a 10-day struggle of alternately clawing against a recurring westerly gale and wallowing in mysterious calms. Not until December 26 did the *Pigeon* finally round the Horn and make ready to start on the next leg of the journey, northward up the west coast of South America.

The *Flying Fish* was not far behind. After his setback in the doldrums, Captain Nickels had made an excellent run south from Cape São Roque. He too opted for the Strait of Le Maire, entering it only five days after the *Pigeon*. Evidently choosing a luckier path that avoided the contrary currents, Nickels got the *Flying Fish* through the passage in a single day, thereby gaining another day on the *Pigeon*.

At about the same time, Captain Doane of the *John Gilpin* chose the outside route. Meeting neither the tides nor the crosscurrents nor the contrary winds that his two competitors had found in the strait, he picked up a strong easterly that sent the *Gilpin* speeding around Staten Island. He reached the Horn on December 27. A few days later he sighted the *Flying Fish*. Aboard both vessels the encounter was an exciting one, and the captains, hoisting their flags, saluted each other. Captain Nickels bellowed through his speaking trumpet, inviting Captain Doane to dinner. Doubtless the invitation was tongue in cheek; the pressures of racing precluded such amenities; in any event the Cape Horn seas were too rough to send a boat between the ships. Captain Doane—joining in the spirit of the moment—bellowed back his polite regrets.

The two vessels lost sight of each other within the day. But both clippers were now neck and neck—and not only with each other, but with the *Wild Pigeon*. All competitors began the northward run up the west coast of South America from the same latitude on the same day. The *Wild Pigeon* still clung to one small advantage; she was farthest west and poised for the straightest, shortest run up north to the California coast. The *John Gilpin* was in the middle, and the *Flying Fish* was closest to the South American coast. As it turned out, the *Pigeon*'s position did not help her much; the same prevailing westerlies sent all three clippers bounding north at the same pace, and on December 30 the *Flying Fish* was within sight of the *Wild Pigeon* as they reached lat. 35° S. The *Pigeon* was now 79 days out of New York, the *Fish* only 59.

Coming up from astern of the *Pigeon*'s counter, Captain Nickels could make out her name with his glass, and he happily recorded the event in his log. The *Pigeon*'s log noted only the appearance of an anonymous clipper ship; the counter of the overtaking vessel was out of Captain

Putnam's line of vision, and he did not imagine that she could be the *Flying Fish*, since she had been scheduled to sail 20 days after he had. And neither captain knew the precise position of the *John Gilpin*; she was, in fact, less than 40 miles astern of them both.

"With fair winds and an open sea," Maury wrote later, "the competitors now had a clear stretch to the equator of two thousand five hundred miles before them." Thundering up this stretch, the *Flying Fish* overtook the *Pigeon*. Still unable to make out the name of the rival ship, Captain Putnam set every sail he had in an attempt to catch up with her. He did not narrow the gap, but he prevented the *Flying Fish* from widening it. For 14 days the two big clippers sliced northward in sight of each other, both bearing straining pyramids of canvas and thrusting their sharp bows through the sparkling green Pacific. Aboard each ship the crewmen alternately squinted across the bright sea at the distant competitor, and then apprehensively watched the groaning spars and iron-hard sails above; the captain, one leg bent to the canting quarter-deck, stood at the weather rail, periodically ordering the first mate to trim a yard or bear up a point. The *John Gilpin*, meanwhile, was still out of sight; Captain Doane had headed off to the west, evidently hoping to find even more wind by going farther out into the Pacific.

When the two leaders reached the Equator on January 13, the *Flying Fish* was still ahead by 25 miles. However, the *Wild Pigeon* had moved 40 miles eastward, toward the South American coast. Captain Putnam, while mindful of Maury's charts, was applying to them some reasoning of his own. The charts showed that the prevailing winds just above the Equator in the winter season were strong northeast trades. It seemed to Putnam that by working in close to the land he would be able to get the most advantage from them; as he ran northwest toward California, he would have them abeam of the ship—or even off his starboard quarter, the most efficient angle of his square-rigged clipper. Meanwhile, his rival, on a more northerly heading in order to lay a line for San Francisco, would be forced to point up into the same winds—a difficult bearing for a square-rigger. Not only would the *Pigeon* have the best slant of wind, she would also be closer to the California coast when the northeast trades gave way to the variable winds off San Francisco, and thus better able to reach into port quickly.

Putnam's idea was perfectly valid, and he had experience as well as Maury's charts to guide him. When he had sailed the *Pigeon* to San Francisco the previous year, he had brought her across the Equator at the same longitude as on this trip, and had enjoyed a highly satisfactory run of only 17 days from the Line to the Farallon Islands off the Golden Gate. But as luck had failed Putnam on the run down the North Atlantic at the outset of this passage, so it failed him now in the Pacific. The *Wild Pigeon* had no sooner crossed the Equator than she stalled in light airs. Captain Putnam waited in vain for the northeast trades to appear. For a week they did not come.

Both the *John Gilpin* and the *Flying Fish* were having better luck. Captain Doane's westward gamble paid off. The *John Gilpin* crossed the Equator on January 15, two days after the two leaders, and then, deep in the Pacific, found a strong northerly on which she dashed to San Fran-

# A long, close run for the victor's laurels

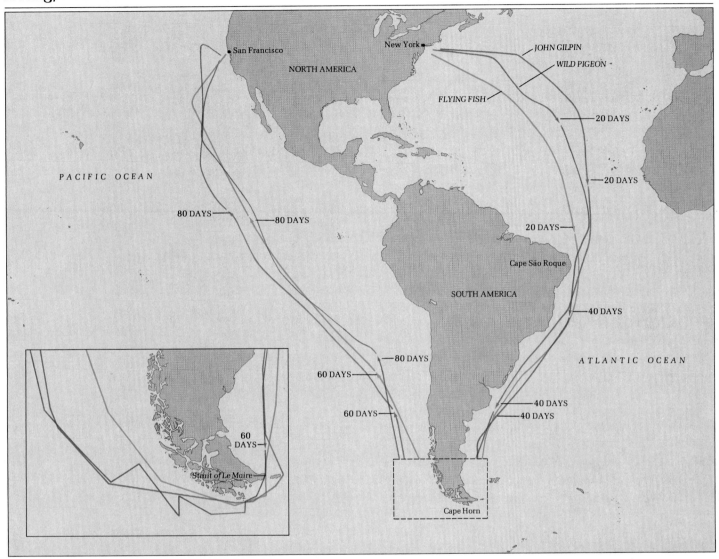

*During the epic three-clipper race to San Francisco in 1852-1853, the Flying Fish left New York last but made the fastest run down the Atlantic, as the elapsed-time points on this chart indicate. She and the Wild Pigeon both doubled Cape Horn by way of the Strait of Le Maire, while the John Gilpin chose the longer but safer route around Staten Island (inset).*

cisco in only 15 days. She arrived there January 31, the first of the fall season's 15 starters to show up, having made the run in the remarkable time of 93 days and 20 hours.

But a day later the *Flying Fish* showed up, topping that score with an elapsed time of 92 days and four hours. Crossing the Equator only 40 miles westward of the *Wild Pigeon*, Captain Nickels had found a belt of the very northeast trade winds that had eluded Captain Putnam closer to shore, and had gone thrashing up to the Golden Gate in 19 days. On February 7, six days behind the *Flying Fish*, the *Wild Pigeon* arrived— after a total passage of 118 days.

The *Wild Pigeon* had been roundly trounced. "Could she have imagined," wrote Maury, "that in consequence of this difference of forty miles in the crossing of the equator, and of the two hours' time behind her competitor, she would fall into a streak of wind which would enable the *Fish* to lead her into port one whole week? Certainly it was nothing but what sailors call a streak of ill luck that could have made such a difference." Gamblers likewise, Maury might have added. No tally survives to attest to the bets that were made, but there is little doubt that many a bundle of money changed hands. And for the fans waiting by the dockyards and in the telegraph offices, the weeks that followed remained exciting as the other 12 of the 15 starters came in one by one.

As for Captain Nickels, he may well have rued the fact that, had he not lost four days by flouting Maury's advice in the doldrums, he might have beaten the 89-day record of the *Flying Cloud*. Even so, he made the best run of the year.

The race brought particular satisfaction to Maury, since it was the first occasion on which his theories had been put to the test by so many vessels sailing the same course at more or less the same time. "Am I far wrong," he asked rhetorically, "when I say that the present state of our knowledge with regard to the physical geography of the sea had enabled the navigator to blaze his way among the winds and currents of the sea, and so mark his path that others, using his signs as fingerboards, may follow in the same track?"

If the virtues of the charts vindicated Maury, the power and speed of the ships themselves reflected on the builders. Altogether the average elapsed time of the 15 ships worked out to 112 days—little more than half the average time of ordinary sailing ships. To the builders, who had been producing clipper ships that were increasingly longer, sleeker and taller of mast, the constantly improving performances seemed to suggest that there was no limit to the marvels that size and tonnage could make possible. No wonder, then, that they went right on building more and more of these dazzling craft, in ever more impressive dimensions. Only 16 clipper ships were produced in 1850, but 44 were built in 1851 and 61 in 1852, and yet another 125 were to come down the ways in 1853.

No shipbuilder worked harder to keep the clippers exceeding their own records than Donald McKay—the man who, as builder of this year's winner, the *Flying Fish*, as well as of the celebrated *Flying Cloud* and the *Westward Ho (pages 10-11)*, had more record holders to his credit than anyone else. The race of 1852 was hardly over before McKay was planning the largest merchant clipper ship that the world had ever seen—and, he hoped, the fastest. Some of his friends protested that the ship would bankrupt him before she was finished. "Let friends and foes talk," McKay retorted; "I'll work"—and he mortgaged everything he had to raise $300,000 to build his dream vessel.

When finished, she had consumed 1.5 million feet of longleaf yellow pine, 2,056 tons of white oak, 336 tons of iron and 56 tons of copper—twice as much material as a United States Navy three-decker warship. At 4,555 tons, she was more than twice the size of any clipper ship that had gone before her. She was as long—335 feet—as a Boston city block. Her mainmast was 44 inches in diameter and soared to a height of 200 feet, as high as one of the new 20-story buildings going up in Manhattan. The first vessel ever to carry more than three masts, she was rigged with four, and they supported 15,653 square yards of canvas, enough to cover a mile of the Boston Post Road.

Sometime before she reached completion, McKay happened to hear

*Seven years after a fire gutted her in 1853 on the eve of her maiden voyage, the rebuilt Great Republic is unloaded at a San Francisco pier. To save on running expenses, her sail plan had been so drastically reduced that she could be managed by a crew half the size of her original 130-man complement. Yet this cutdown giant among clippers still won rapturous praise. One admirer wrote: "She can scarcely find a sea wide enough, with belts of wind broad enough for the full display of her qualities and capabilities."*

the popular actress Fanny Kemble read a new poem by Henry Wadsworth Longfellow called "The Building of the Ship" that metaphorically celebrated the rise of the young United States as a great republic. According to a grandson, the experience so profoundly moved McKay that it inspired the name for the vessel he had under construction. Discarding the recent fashion for names suggesting airy fleetness, he called his new masterpiece the *Great Republic.*

The public shared McKay's excitement. October 4, 1853, her launching date, was declared a Massachusetts holiday. Whole schools arrived in chartered hayracks. Families came from Cape Ann and as far away as Cape Cod in horse-drawn carriages and ox-drawn carts. The harbor was jammed with sloops, yachts and small boats. Cannon boomed, church bells pealed and 50,000 people cheered as the Gargantuan new vessel was christened and slipped down the ways into Boston harbor. McKay had planned to have the rite performed in the traditional way, with champagne. But in a prelaunch celebration the night before, his eldest son and some yard foremen had consumed all the champagne. So, improvising at the last moment, McKay used drinking water instead—a fact that a number of Boston ladies took as a nod to the temperance movement. McKay made no attempt to disabuse them of this notion.

The ceremonies over, the *Great Republic* was towed to New York, where Donald McKay's brother Lauchlan supervised the installation of her masts, yards and rigging. In New York she was as much a cynosure as in Boston; for the next two months, while she lay at an East River pier at the foot of Dover Street, crowds flocked to admire her—among them the Governor and members of the New York State Legislature, who made the 150-mile trip down from Albany just for the purpose.

By the day after Christmas, the work was completed. The *Great Republic's* massive sails were bent on, and her 6,000-ton hold was filled with a cargo of wheat for Liverpool, whither she was to sail within the week.

Tragedy struck sometime toward midnight on December 26. A fire started at the Novelty Bakery on nearby Front Street. A gale was blowing, and flying sparks from the bakery ignited the *Great Republic's* sails. By the time Lauchlan McKay had been roused and had rushed to the pier, he found a holocaust. The *Great Republic* was burning aloft like a forest fire, and nearly a dozen other ships nearby were ablaze as well. The fire department was already in action, but its hoses could not send water any higher than the lowest of the *Great Republic's* lofty yardarms, and the water sloshed about the deck instead. A few brave volunteers went aboard to chop down the burning masts, but to no avail; the rain of flaming canvas and burning blocks drove everyone back to the pier.

By now the whole waterfront was in jeopardy, and the only recourse was to move the fire itself. So the *Great Republic's* mooring lines were cast off and a tug pulled her into the river. There she sat and burned for two days. By that time the water that had missed the rigging aloft had seeped below to the hold, where it soaked the grain, which swelled and ruptured the seams of the hull. Then the yardarms, still burning, gave way and fell hissing into the river; the *Great Republic* groaned, lurched and sank, settling in the mud of New York Harbor.

For Donald McKay, the burning of the *Great Republic* was a shattering blow, and he had no heart for beginning all over again to re-create her. So he signed over the waterlogged hull to the insurer, recouped his full financial investment and—presumably on the theory that bigness for its own sake had gone as far as it could go—turned his attention to ships of more modest design. In the remaining 27 years of his life, he was to build another 38 vessels; among them, besides more clippers, were barks, schooners, down-easters (*pages 164-171*) and gunboats for the United States Navy. Every one was to prove strong, swift and durable. But they would set few racing records.

The underwriters of the *Great Republic*, meanwhile, found a buyer in the firm of A. A. Low & Bro., which had her rebuilt under the supervision of Captain Nathaniel Palmer, the designer of the *Houqua*. He had her hull made 1,200 tons smaller, and cut down her rigging, keeping her four masts but reducing their height by one quarter and shortening the yards proportionately. Even then she remained the largest merchantman afloat. When, on March 15, 1855, she arrived in London, her first port of call on her maiden voyage, she had to anchor in the middle of the Thames because no pier had enough water alongside to take her.

Of more concern to her new owner and all other clipper-ship admirers was her speed. Would her great hull and towering rigging enable her to

## A costly war for American clippers

During the Civil War the American clipper-ship business—already hurt by a devastating economic slump in the late 1850s and by competition from steamships—received a final, mortal blow from a handful of Confederate cruisers. The most successful of these wooden steamers were built in England, and—because of British dependence on Confederate cotton—all were covertly supported in their raids by the British government, despite its avowed neutrality.

The speedy cruisers gave chase to every merchantman they sighted, fired a shot across the ship's bow and then sent a boatload of armed men swarming aboard. If the vessel proved to be registered abroad, the boarding party quickly apologized and departed. If the ship was American, the boarders took the crew prisoner, looted the prize, then put a torch to it. "The flames could be heard roaring like the fires of a hundred furnaces in full blast," wrote one Confederate captain after a successful mission.

Although the raiders actually destroyed only 14 clippers among the 150 or so merchant ships they burned, the indirect effects were disastrous. Panic,

outrace the 300 clipper ships now afloat? The *Great Republic* spent the next 17 years sailing most of the seven seas. Once, in 1857, she made a record 16-day run from New York to the Equator. In the same year she equaled the *Flying Fish's* 92-day run to San Francisco; she was thus tied for fourth place on that run, following the famous *Flying Cloud* (twice at 89 days) and two other clippers, the *Andrew Jackson* and the *Sword Fish*, which had logged 89 and 90 days, respectively. In sum, the *Great Republic* proved to be a swift but not an outstanding clipper ship. Some of her champions held that if she had sailed with her original hull and rigging she would surely have exceeded the speed of any ship afloat. But since her original specifications were never put to the test, that possibility remained hypothetical.

In 1857 the young United States slid into a severe economic depression. Nowhere was it more evident than in maritime affairs. The tonnage of American cargo sold in foreign countries fell from 65,000 in 1855 to 42,000 in 1856; by 1860 it had plunged to 17,000 tons, a drop of 75 per cent in just five years. Traffic between American ports also slowed. The territory of California was now producing its own wheat, tools and clothing, and thus was no longer completely dependent on imports from the East Coast. And by 1860 the United States had 30,000 miles of railroad tracks, which were carrying much of the nation's freight. Shipbuilding came to a near standstill.

In England, meanwhile, clipper-ship construction had expanded. By 1860 the *Chrysolite* and the *Stornoway* had been followed by 18 sister ships. As their own fleet of clippers grew, British merchants no longer chartered American clippers to bring their tea from China—thus adding to the woes of American shipowners. In 1860 the new nation suffered another blow—civil war, which immobilized her maritime trade for another four years. By the time the War had ended, Britain's primacy in clipper building and the China trade was unassailable.

By comparison with their American forerunners, British clippers were diminutive, typically about 1,000 tons—as compared with 2,000 tons for an average American clipper in the late 1850s. They had less curvature from bow to stern, lower bulwarks and plumper waists. And though they never achieved such astonishing bursts of speed as the 22 knots the *Sovereign of the Seas* made on some stretches, the British clippers were considerably better in light winds. Averaging about 15⅛ knots, they could be counted on to make the run home from China in about 110 days.

If the British had been reluctant suitors of the clipper ship at first, they now conducted a love affair as ardent as the Americans' had been. No other vessel commanded such devotion from builders and captains, and none so caught the fancy of merchants and the public. The tea merchants devised an incentive system that did much to ensure that clippers performed up to their potential; they offered an annual premium of 10 shillings per ton to the owner of the first vessel to dock with the season's new tea. On a million-pound cargo of tea, the total premium amounted to about £2,500. The shipowners passed £100 of that on to their captains, who normally earned only about twice that much each year.

Predictably, British captains went to almost any length to win, and

fanned by bold Confederate forays into the very mouth of New York Harbor, swept through Union shipping circles. Premiums for war-risk insurance rose out of all proportion to actual losses, and ships with neutral flags soon wrested away much of the business that had supported United States vessels. Desperate American owners rushed to sell their ships abroad—usually at discount prices. By 1865 more than 1,600 vessels, including virtually all of the American merchant fleet's proud clippers, had been transferred to foreign owners. The remainder of the fleet consisted primarily of obsolescent tubs.

Seven years after the War, an international tribunal ordered Britain to pay reparations of $15.5 million for its complicity with the Confederate raiders—a paltry price for the merchant-shipping gains the British had won at American expense. The United States merchant fleet did not recover until after World War I.

*Dense smoke pours from the doomed Union clipper Harvey Birch as raiders from the Confederate side-wheeler Nashville row away with the clipper's captured crew.*

stories about the tricks they played on one another provided many a sailor's yarn. According to one tale, Captain John Care of the clipper *Lord Macaulay* was approaching a narrow passage in the Java Sea at sundown when he sighted the *Elizabeth Nicholson*, a new ship in the hands of a novice commander, coming up astern. Captain Care instantly began to shorten sail as if he intended to lay to for the night; he was pleased to see that the crew of the *Elizabeth Nicholson* began to do the same. His own crew, in on the plan he had in mind, cooperated by dallying over the *Lord Macaulay*'s sails until the *Elizabeth Nicholson* drew near enough for the captain's voice to be heard. Then Captain Care bellowed loudly: "Stand by and let go the anchor." Again his own crew cooperatively fumbled while they waited to hear the splash of the *Nicholson*'s anchor, and then—undetected in the darkness that had now fallen—they set their sails and slipped through the channel. By morning, when the *Elizabeth Nicholson*'s gullible captain was up and about, the *Lord Macaulay* had stolen a lead of 70 miles.

Another skipper, Captain Jacob D. Whitmore of the *Sea Serpent*, hatched an even more devious scheme. After bringing his clipper from China as far as Plymouth, he disembarked there, boarded a train for London and declared his ship as having arrived—while he left to his officers and crew the job of actually bringing her up the Thames. His ingenuity came to nought: Two other clippers, the *Fiery Cross* and the *Ellen Rodger*, had already docked legitimately.

Those two pranks were harmless enough, but occasionally a racing trick might lead to disaster. Captain Anthony Enright, who commanded the *Chrysolite* for a good many years, was once on a passage home from China when, off the island of Banca in the China Sea, he came up alongside the American clipper *Memnon*. The master of the *Memnon*, a China-trade neophyte named Joseph Gordon, hailed the *Chrysolite* and inquired of Captain Enright if he intended to go across Macclesfield Bank that night. The bank was a shortcut for a captain who knew the way but—because of its reefs and rocky islands—was a perilous route for one who did not. While the two captains were conferring, the passengers aboard the *Chrysolite* (among whom were a party of Americans) began placing bets on which of the two ships would reach London first. Captain Enright, who made a point of abstaining from gambling on the ground that it was sinful, declined to join in the passengers' wagering—but yielded to temptation of another kind. To Captain Gordon's question he replied that indeed he was going through Macclesfield Bank, knowing full well that Captain Gordon would try to follow and that his inexperience was likely to get him into trouble.

*Decked out in their Sunday best, the key craftsmen and clerks of Alexander Hall and Sons, renowned Aberdeen shipbuilders, assemble for an 1862 portrait with chief designer William Hall (back row, fourth from right) and his brother James (back row, second from right), the shipyard manager. Twenty-three years earlier, the talented Hall brothers had introduced an extremely raked, clipper-like bow on their ships, and they held the lead in the construction of British clippers for decades.*

Night fell, a squall came up and, before long, both ships were obscured in the darkness and the rain. But the *Chrysolite* sailed steadily on, with Captain Enright himself at the wheel, while the *Memnon* went aground on a sharp coral reef, tearing a hole in her hull. In vain the *Memnon's* crewmen tried to bail her out, but the hole was too big. By daylight a horde of Malay pirates had swarmed aboard and stripped the ship of everything valuable, and Captain Gordon and his crew had fled in three boats, lucky to escape with their lives. Captain Enright was by this time speeding the *Chrysolite* toward England, with nary a thought for his luckless fellow captain.

In falling victim to both piracy and the reefs, Captain Gordon had been initiated into two of the commonest hazards of the China trade. Pirates lurked everywhere on the shores of the China Sea, swarming out in innocent-looking fishing boats to prey upon the rich cargo-laden vessels of the Western traders. In the year 1853 nearly 700 ships were plundered in the Hong Kong area alone. Clipper ships went armed with as many as four guns, but they were usually useless; more often than not, the pirates descended when a ship's crewmen were preoccupied with an accident such as the one that had befallen Captain Gordon.

As for reefs and shoals, they abounded in the China Sea, and were poorly mapped: China's waters had not yet been charted by Maury. To compound the navigational problems, most of the tea ports lay miles upriver. The worst of all the rivers was the Min, which cut a twisting 25-mile course through tall canyons to the port of Foochow. In some places it was so narrow that, according to old China hands, monkeys jumped across it—getting their tails tangled in the clippers' upper rigging. And almost everywhere it was filled with swift currents that went by the onomatopoeic name of *chow-chow* in Chinese. The *chow-chow* currents could dash the vessel of an unwary skipper onto any of hundreds of hidden sandbanks and rocky shores.

To negotiate the rivers, the clipper-ship captains had to rely on pilots, who left a lot to be desired. Most of them were European expatriates, probably former seamen who found life in the China ports more congenial than life aboard a hard-working ship. Many had a weakness for alcohol. Perhaps the most notorious drunk among them was a fellow named Hughie Sutherland. When a clipper captain found Hughie drinking milk one morning, he shook his head and said: "Too late, Hughie, too late." But Hughie was a valuable ally when on his mettle; it was said he could save a racing ship as much as a day in the run down the Min.

By 1860 Foochow had replaced Canton as the major tea port, largely because the tea that grew in the surrounding province of Fukien was harvested in May and June, two months earlier than anywhere else in China. Thus clippers sailing from Foochow not only had a head start for England but avoided the worst of the southwest monsoons, which buffeted the China Sea throughout July and August.

Few marinas in the world were more colorful than Foochow's Pagoda Anchorage, a harbor shaped like a clover leaf and nestled below verdant hillsides studded with temples. In the 1860s a dozen and more tall clippers gathered there every spring to wait for the year's harvest, riding their anchors in the bay, their slim spars precisely parallel, their mast-

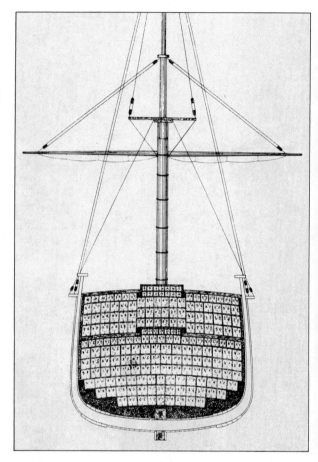

*A diagram drawn by a naval architect in the 1860s shows how ships in the tea trade stuffed chests into almost every cubic inch of their holds, packing oddly shaped spaces with half chests and small so-called catty boxes. The Chinese laborers who loaded the ships were so skilled, noted one captain, that the surface of the hold looked "like a splendid deck, flush from stem to stern."*

heads stabbing the sky and their brightwork flashing in the sun. By late May sampans were bringing the tea downstream from the plantations that lined the banks for 100 miles upriver. As soon as they arrived, armies of coolies transferred the tea chests from the sampans to the clippers bound for London.

Once the loading began, it went on at a feverish pace for two or three days around the clock, with no rest on Sundays—and no loafing on the job. Some of the captains stationed their ships' boys in the hold, armed with bamboo poles to smack any loader tempted to dawdle.

Loading a clipper was a fine art. Tea was such a light cargo that a great deal of ballast had to be carried to keep the slender vessel steady. At the bottom of the hold went about 100 tons of kentledge—scrap iron culled from the foundries of England's industrial cities. Depending on the size of the clipper and the amount of the tea cargo, as much as 200 tons of beach pebbles might be stowed above the kentledge for further ballast. Both ballast and cargo had to be packed tight to keep them from shifting at sea; the trim of the ship was vital to her speed, and an inch too much or too little at bow or stern could slow her down by a knot.

A floor of planking was laid over the ballast, and then came the tea, in straw-covered wooden chests and half chests—the latter an innovation of recent years, when it was realized that more half chests could be packed into nooks and crannies than the older full chests. The inferior teas were placed on the bottom layers, and the better teas on top, away from souring bilge water if the ship should leak. Every chest was hammered into place so that not a hair's breadth of space remained between them. More stone and pebble were forced in where the straightedged chests met the curved hull.

When the last chest was in place, a blanket of split bamboo and canvas was laid over the top layer, canted so that any sea water sloshing into the hold would drain along the sides of the hull. The hatches were closed and sealed, and the clipper's anchor clanked aboard. Her topsails were loosed, and a steam tug towed her downriver through the high gorges for the open sea and the race to London.

Of all the races that took place in the decade and a half when clipper ships were in their prime, none caused such a stir as the one that Englishmen were to remember as the Great Tea Race of 1866. An unprecedented 16 clippers assembled at the Pagoda Anchorage that year to vie for the 10-shilling-per-ton premium promised the winner. Of the 16 ships, five were stellar performers.

One was the *Serica*, a 708-ton vessel launched in 1863 and commanded by Captain George Innes. Another was the 767-ton *Taeping*, under Captain Donald McKinnon; on her maiden voyage the preceding year, she had come in second. Still another contender was the *Fiery Cross*, an 888-ton vessel that under her present commander, Captain Richard Robinson, had won four out of the five races since 1861. And there was the 815-ton *Taitsing*, noted for her exquisite teak and mahogany woodwork throughout, and under Captain Daniel Nutsford the object of much attention because she was on her maiden voyage. Rounding out the favorites was the *Ariel*, a slender beauty of 853 tons, with so much brass that

four men had to polish it from 6 a.m. till 6 p.m. daily to keep it shining properly. She was one year old and had already proved a smart sailer. "I could trust her like a thing alive," Captain John Keay was to write of her. She was also the odds-on favorite with the public.

The new tea began coming downriver to the Pagoda Anchorage on Thursday, May 24, and by Sunday the 27th hundreds of lighters crowded the harbor, 16 of them clustered around the *Ariel.* All that day and through the night the clippers loaded, and by 2 p.m. on Monday the *Ariel* was ready, with 1,230,900 pounds of tea aboard.

Three hours after the last tea chest had been thumped into place, the *Ariel* raised anchor and the steam tug *Island Queen* took her towline to lead her down the twisting course of the Min River. She was first off the mark, but she scarcely had time to relish the fact before she suffered a tragicomic mishap. The paddler *Island Queen* was one of the clumsiest in China; one observer pronounced her "no good except in still water." Sure enough, the *Island Queen* got caught in a *chow-chow* current, and while all aboard the *Ariel* watched in grim frustration the *Fiery Cross,* towed by a swifter tug, slipped past and took the lead. Then the *Ariel* lost more precious time when a boat capsized while returning the pilot and his aides to the *Island Queen*; the latter's crew took so long to save the floundering men that the *Ariel* had to signal for another pilot boat to come to their rescue. When the tug *Island Queen* finally cast the *Ariel* loose at the river mouth on the morning of Wednesday, May 30, the *Fiery Cross* was already hull down on the China Sea; the *Taeping* and the *Serica* had caught up with the *Ariel*, and the *Taitsing* was making her way downriver not far behind. The remaining 11 vessels were to sail one at a time over the next weeks, but none would worry the five leaders.

Of the whole 15,000-mile regatta, the first leg—the 2,500-mile stretch from the mouth of the Min to the Sunda Strait—was the most difficult. The southwest monsoon was beginning to blow up, alternating calms and squalls as the wind veered erratically and unpredictably from one point of the compass to another.

Aboard the *Ariel*, Captain Keay found that his vessel was badly out of trim—down at the bow. He ordered 30 fathoms of anchor chain dragged aft to shift the weight to the stern. When that proved insufficient to make her right, he shifted 16 chests and 23 half chests out of the hold and into his cabin. Still not satisfied, he instructed the ship's carpenter to build a large box and fill it with kentledge, spare anchors and coal; this would serve as portable ballast that could be moved about the ship to help keep her in trim as she changed from one tack to another.

Captain Keay lost sight of his four competitors on June 1, soon after they entered upon the broad China Sea. The *Taeping* came back into view nine days later, and the next day Captain Keay noted in his log: "*Taeping* about four miles on our lee quarter." Captain McKinnon signaled across a friendly message that the *Taeping* had passed the *Fiery Cross* two days earlier; so Keay recorded, "We are thus in all probability the headmost ship so far."

With all studding sails set, the *Ariel* raced south and reached the Sunda Strait 21 days out of Foochow. At Anyer Lor Captain Keay paused only long enough to send up flags to signal his position to authorities ashore; then he dashed on without even waiting to learn that he was not the leader after all: The *Fiery Cross* had passed through the strait the day before. On the other side of the strait, a steady breeze came from the east-southeast. Every sail went up, and the *Ariel* flew out across the Indian Ocean. The *Taeping*, the *Serica* and the *Taitsing* passed through the strait during the next five days, and the news was duly cabled from Java to a rapt public in England.

Crossing the Indian Ocean, the five clippers bent on all canvas, leaned their narrow hulls into the green seas and ran westward for Mauritius, their next mark before heading south to round the Cape of Good Hope. It was wet work. Keay's log reported on June 25: "Shipping water over all these two days past." It was also taxing to the ships; two of the *Ariel*'s topmasts broke under the strain. Like any driving captain, Keay had them fixed on the run, and the *Ariel* pressed on with little loss of time.

This was usually the fastest stretch for China clippers, since they rode steady and strong southeast trade winds. It was also the most exhilarating part of the passage, with the spray flashing under the tropical sun and the heady excitement of sweeping by ordinary merchantmen. One day the men aboard the *Ariel* saw the East Indiaman *City of Bombay*, also

*Riding so high that their copper hull sheathing glints above the placid water, empty clippers gather at the Pagoda Anchorage on China's Min River to load up for the 1866 tea race back to London. The ships carried general cargo from England to Shanghai or Hong Kong during the winter and then sailed in ballast to this anchorage below Foochow, gathering early in May to load the area's first tea harvest of the year.*

en route to London, come into view ahead at noon; four hours later the *Ariel* had left her far astern.

But out of sight of the rival clippers, Keay and his crew had only their knowledge of past records by which to estimate their standing in the race, and they were never free of the anxious concern that, even if they were ahead of the record, any of their competitors might be farther ahead yet. Indeed, when the *Ariel* was off Mauritius by July 1, only 11 days from Java, Captain Keay had no way of knowing that she was a day behind the *Fiery Cross*. Nevertheless, when on August 4 she reached the Equator, she crossed the Line simultaneously with the *Fiery Cross*—and with the *Taeping*. Both ships were invisible over the horizon. The race was now a three-way tie.

The clippers raced on for another month, passing up the coast of Africa, through the Azores, into the Bay of Biscay and on to the English Channel. In the first week of September came a breathtaking finish.

At 1:30 a.m. on September 5, Captain Keay sighted Bishop and St. Agnes Lights on the south coast of England. The night was stormy, slowing down the *Ariel*, but at dawn the sky cleared and a strong wind came out of the west-southwest. Tasting the prize bone in his teeth, Keay set all possible sail and sent the *Ariel* skimming up the English Channel. Before the day was over he saw one of his rivals off his starboard quarter. She was too far away for him to read her name, but her tall sails and the easy grace with which she was gliding through the water marked her clearly as a tea clipper. Keay said afterward, "Instinct told me that it was the *Taeping*." It was.

Throughout the day of September 5, while sailors aboard other vessels in the Channel and spectators along the English coast looked on in fascination, the two clippers fought out the last leg of the journey. Both captains sent up every sail in their ships' lockers. The two towering clouds of canvas chased each other through the flashing chop of the Channel, with the wind-swept spray flying to the yardarms. Slicing ahead at 14 knots, the *Ariel* continued to hold the lead, but the *Taeping* gained on her hour by hour.

At sunset the two clippers were passing the Isle of Wight. On through the dark night they plunged, all sails straining in ghostly white clouds above them and white bow spray regularly blotting out the navigation lights along the coast. At midnight Captain Keay saw Beachy Head; by 3 a.m. he could make out Dungeness Light, where the clippers would take on their pilots. By 4 a.m. the *Ariel* had reached that point, and Keay took in some of his sail and hove to. Then he fired a series of rockets to signal for a pilot. The sky exploded above him and a profusion of colors showered down from the heavens into the water.

For Keay and his crewmen, an anxious hour followed while they waited on deck, their shadows dancing as the flares continued to burst in the air and fizzle in the dark sea. As they watched, the *Taeping* came heaving up. She too sent flare rockets arcing into the air. But instead of shortening sail, she continued to move steadily on in the direction of Dungeness harbor.

Keay guessed that Captain McKinnon was taking the *Taeping* closer to Dungeness in a bid to pick up the first pilot to put out from the harbor.

Inasmuch as the *Ariel* had arrived off Dungeness first, Keay had no intention of letting McKinnon slip the *Taeping* in ahead of him. Swiftly appraising the situation, he called for more sail and commanded the helmsman to steer northeastward, a maneuver that would take the *Ariel* straight across the *Taeping*'s bow and put her closer to the harbor. Now it was McKinnon's turn to take alarm aboard the *Taeping*. Watching the silent apparition bearing down on his ship and threatening to ram, he knew he had no choice but to head up into the wind and slow down to avoid a collision.

The *Ariel* glided past the *Taeping*—just in time to meet the first of two cutters now pitching out from the harbor. A moment later the pilot scrambled aboard, saluted Captain Keay and congratulated him on being the first one in from China.

"We have not room to boast yet," Keay replied, and set all plain sail—the basic array of canvas carried in ordinary weather—as the *Ariel* made ready to move on. They indeed had no room to boast, for the other cutter had already reached the *Taeping*, and soon it was apparent that McKinnon had set more than plain sail; the *Taeping* had studding sails fluttering on the starboard side—and she was gaining on the *Ariel*. As Keay watched McKinnon close the distance between the two ships to a mile, he prepared to set his studding sails too. Then he changed his mind. When the clippers ran around the tip of Kent, as they were soon to do, the course would change from east to north, and Keay calculated that the *Taeping*'s studding sails would then lose their wind. They did, and moments later Keay could see the men of McKinnon's crew try to set them on the port, or windward, side. But the angle was too close; the sails did not draw, and shortly they came fluttering down. The *Ariel* maintained her slim lead.

Next the two clippers crossed the Downs. Here both captains took in most of their sails and sent their numbers to their mastheads, signaling to the authorities at Deal harbor that they were ready for steam tugs to tow them to the Thames and thence to London. The *Ariel* was still a mile ahead of the *Taeping*, but at the 14-knot speed they were going, that was only eight minutes of lead time—after a 15,000-mile passage of 99 days.

To the tea merchants and the betting public waiting in London, the race had yet a little way to go. The contest would not be decided until the tea was unloaded and on the dock. There still remained an element of chance between now and that final moment—and now chance began to favor the *Taeping*.

In his zeal to get the first tug that entered the Thames, Captain Keay had the same bad luck he had had when exiting from the Min; he got another inferior vessel. Keay and his crewmen looked on with dismay as the *Taeping* slipped past the *Ariel*. It seemed that the jig was up.

Suddenly Keay had an inspiration. He made a quick calculation and concluded that both clippers would reach Gravesend, the mouth of the Thames, when the tide was out. There would not be enough water in the river for them to enter, nor for a couple of hours would either of them be able to proceed upriver to the London wharves. He swiftly formed a plan.

The *Taeping* and her tug sped on; the *Ariel* slowed down imperceptibly but signaled for a second tug. The *Taeping* reached Gravesend 55

minutes ahead of the *Ariel* and, as Keay had anticipated, McKinnon anchored. Keay, by holding back the *Ariel*, managed to creep up to the mouth of the Thames just as the tide began to turn. Then, while the *Taeping's* crew labored to haul in the anchor, the *Ariel* swept right on up the river behind her pair of tugs.

Keay had remembered another point in the *Ariel's* favor; her destination, the East India Dock, was farther downriver than the *Taeping's* London dock. And so by 9 p.m. the *Ariel* was off the East India Dock, and Keay and his crewmen watched with satisfaction as the *Taeping* was towed past them up the Thames. They had every reason to think themselves the winners at last.

Not yet; the tide was still too low for the *Ariel* to warp alongside the East India Dock and throw the first tea chests ashore. Keay and his crew waited an exasperating hour and 23 minutes to do so. Meanwhile, the *Taeping*, which drew slightly less water, was able to tie up at her more distant dock at 10 o'clock sharp. Now Captain McKinnon and all aboard the *Taeping*, learning that the *Ariel* was still waiting to dock, had their moment for self-congratulation.

*Laboring around the clock, British stevedores trundle tea chests into an East India Dock warehouse and stack them to the ceiling, while a derrick lowers more chests to the wharf. A ship could be emptied of a million pounds of tea in little more than a day, and Liverpool and Manchester retail shops were often selling new tea the morning after the arrival of a vessel at the docks in London.*

*Two weeks after a glut of tea delivered in the 1866 race knocked the bottom out of an already depressed London tea market, this poster appeared, advertising retail discounts on the new tea. The five leading clippers (the advertisement omits one, the Taitsing) actually delivered much less tea than the poster indicates, about 5.2 million pounds, or approximately 5 per cent of the annual consumption in the United Kingdom.*

# GREAT RACE
OF THE
# TEA SHIPS,
WITH THE FIRST
## NEW SEASON'S TEAS.

## PRICE OF TEAS REDUCED.

THE "Taeping," "Ariel," "Fiery Cross," and "Serica" have arrived, with others in close pursuit, with something like **FORTY-FIVE MILLION POUNDS** of **NEW TEA** on board—half a year's consumption for the **United Kingdom.** This enormous weight coming suddenly into the London Docks, Shippers are compelled to submit to **MUCH LOWER PRICES,** in order to make sales.

**We are thus enabled to make a Reduction of FOURPENCE in the pound.**

4/0 down to - - 3/8
3/8 „ - - 3/4
3/4 „ - - 3/0
**And so on downwards.**

We may add the above Ships have brought a few lots of most unusual fine quality.

**Reduction takes place on Friday the 21st inst.**

155, OXFORD STREET;
57, STRETFORD ROAD;
171, STRETFORD ROAD—
"Great Northern." } **BURGON & CO.,**
*TEA MERCHANTS.*

Actually, fate and the owners of the vessels had played the gallant men of both vessels a cruel trick. Unbeknownst to them, tea prices in London had taken a steep and sudden dive in the months during which they were reaching home; too many million pounds of tea were about to descend on London. The tea merchants were now regretting the open-handed promise they had made in a happier past, and the shipowners were looking grimly to the future. It occurred to the owners of the *Ariel,* Shaw, Maxton & Co., and to those of the *Taeping,* Rodger & Co., that in the event of a dispute over the results of the race the merchants might have an excuse to withdraw the prize altogether. So on receiving telegrams from Deal bearing the news that the two clippers had arrived off the Downs, members of both companies hurriedly held a clandestine meeting in London. They agreed that they had nothing to lose and everything to gain by reaching a quiet understanding. They therefore pledged that the clipper that docked first should be publicly declared the winner of the merchants' premium without protest from the opponent, and that the winner would discreetly divide the premium with the loser. The £100 bonus promised by the owners themselves would similarly be split between the captains of the two clippers.

The official verdict was announced by the tea merchants on the following morning, September 7. The *Taeping* was the victor. The owners repaired to the Ship and Turtle tavern on Leadenhall Street with their captains and divided up the prize.

The solution made nobody happy. Though Captain Keay and his crew got half the prize they did not have the glory of public acclamation, and though Captain McKinnon and his men had the public honor they reaped only half the winner's prize. The public, even without knowing of the owners' collusion, was no more satisfied with the official result. In the days and weeks following the race, arguments raged in the press and in private clubrooms over the criteria by which the race had been judged. Partisans of the *Ariel* found it monstrously unfair that, having been the first to reach Deal, she had not been acclaimed the winner; no feats of seamanship were required once the tugs took over. Others held that the *Taeping,* by docking first, had fulfilled the requirements of the race; it was the delivery of the tea, after all, that counted with the merchants, who had put up the ante. Private bettors were left to fight out the issue for themselves.

Meanwhile, the three runners-up had come in right behind the two winners. The *Serica* arrived on the same tide as the *Ariel* and the *Taeping* on September 6 and tied up at 11:30 p.m.—just before the dock gates closed for the night. Two days later came the *Fiery Cross* and the *Taitsing,* logging 101 days each.

The first five ships landed 5,241,202 pounds of fresh tea in London within two days. As the other clippers straggled in with 11 million tons more, prices were depressed still further. Such a state of affairs inevitably cooled the ardor of the merchants, who suspended the premiums the following year. Notwithstanding that mournful anticlimax, the British public endowed the Great Tea Race of 1866 with a kind of immortality; it was the closest match in clipper-racing history, and a thrilling display of the expertise of shipbuilders, captains and crewmen alike.

# A passenger's view of a "most pleasant voyage"

"Our ship must be a magnificent sight, like some very large seabird," wrote clipper passenger Alfred Withers in 1857. "We to a great extent lose the effect." But to Withers, the excitement of traveling aboard a clipper more than made up for missing the visual effect.

His ship was the *James Baines*, one of the few clippers designed primarily as passenger vessels. Withers, emigrating from England to Australia with his bride, kept a diary of his trip and illustrated it with watercolor sketches. It provides a fascinating passenger's-eye-view of life on a clipper.

Seven days out, the ship ran into "a perfect hurricane," Withers recorded. "The sails which were not furled blew away with a noise like a cannon, boxes and chests afloat below, bedding saturated, ladies in hysterics."

But several days later, in fine weath-er, there was "no more motion than if one was sitting in a parlor at home." Life on board settled down to a peaceful routine. The passengers organized amusement committees, danced and attended church services on deck, and had dinner with the captain at his table ("a very stiff formal affair, plenty of *iced* champagne").

Even for first-class passengers like Withers, the voyage had minor hardships; fresh water was rationed except when rainfall offered relief. "I succeeded in catching sufficient water to fill all our pans and baths," Withers wrote after a storm; "this is a great luxury." But inconveniences were less common on a swift and comfortable clipper than on most ships, and Withers concluded that his 82-day passage on the *James Baines* was "the most pleasant voyage I have had."

*As a paddle-wheel steam tug turns back toward Liverpool, the 226-foot, 2,275-ton James Baines finally gets under way. The overland part of the Witherses' journey—noted in the diary entry below the painting—was now behind them and, Withers wrote, "the report of two guns over our heads told us that the voyage had really begun."*

*Withers' wife, Madge, and her female traveling companion sit huddled on a stone quay, from which a steamer would take them to the James Baines, anchored a mile away in Liverpool's Mersey River. "We had to wait four hours exposed to a sharp cold wind and rain, perched on the luggage enveloped in rugs, shawls and umbrellas," wrote Withers. But the ladies, he said, "bore it bravely."*

Tug Steamer leaving the "James Baines" on her Outward Voyage
off Liverpool January 5th 1857

We left London January 2 1857 and arrived at
Liverpool 9 PM, deposited our Luggage at the Cloak
Room, after which bent our Steps to the "Angel Hotel"
had Tea which we all enjoyed and then to Bed.
January 3rd. Breakfast at 8 after which to the
Station for our Luggage, thence to the Old Seacombe
Slip or pier, where the Steamer conveying the
Passengers and Luggage Starts from for the "James
Baines" at Anchor one mile up the River, the
scene on the pier no one can realize unless they

"Madge was soon quite at home here," Withers wrote of their tidy little cabin. "In two hours our drawers, boxes and every movable article became fixtures by screwing them to the floor and bulkheads so that they couldn't move by the rolling of the ship and everything was made snug for the bad weather."

The first-class dining room was planned for meals taken in heavy seas: Benches were set in the walls, and bottles and glasses were held in racks. But these measures were not always enough. Wrote Withers of dining in a storm: "A boiled leg of mutton leaps off the dish like a flying fish onto a gentleman's shirt front, a beef steak pie clings fondly to the heart of another, the mustard potatoes etc. being evenly distributed amongst the remainder of the table."

A passenger stares glumly from the ratlines, where he has been tied by sailors who caught him climbing there. The seamen took unkindly to having their territory aloft invaded by passengers who, as Withers put it, "aspire to raise themselves above their fellow creatures by ascending the rigging." Transgressors might be kept there until a bottle of rum was offered to the crew as atonement.

"Below is a rough but true sketch of a funeral at sea," wrote Withers of his picture of Captain Charles McDonnell reading a service for a child. The bereaved father stands by as two sailors prepare to lower the flag-draped coffin into the sea. Withers said the boy "fell against one of the spars on deck and injured his head, he also had an attack of bronchitis, the two combined caused his death."

Passengers, probably participating in the ship's pool for guessing the arrival time in Melbourne, study a newly posted report showing the position of the vessel. The captain generally published the James Baines's latitude and longitude daily "after taking the sun." Noted Withers: "The excitement to see how much we have done is tremendous."

Standing near a coiled rope on deck, Captain McDonnell takes a sighting of the sun with his sextant. Withers confided to his journal: "I like him very much, he is a first-rate sailor, gentlemanly in behavior and keeps everybody in their proper distance, he is very strict with the men, and will have the rules of the ship enforced among the passengers."

Taking a log-line reading, a sailor eyes an hourglass as two others hold a reel playing out a line that a fourth feeds over the side. The men determined the vessel's speed by measuring the distance a piece of wood tied to the line traveled in the water before the sand ran out. The James Baines was said to have a top speed of 21 knots, and once covered 423 miles in 24 hours.

Chickens, which provided eggs for the pantry, peek out of their coop on the afterdeck, while passengers lounge nearby and a sailor stands duty at the wheel. The wheelhouse behind the helmsman served as a lockup for unruly seamen and passengers alike. In it, Captain McDonnell "made room for five second class passengers who are punished for playing cards all night with a candle stuck in the blankets." Concluded Withers, "Serves them right."

# Chapter 5

# "A grand ship that will last forever"

According to an ancient legend spun in the brooding Scottish countryside—and later turned into verse by the poet Robert Burns—a farmer named Tam o'Shanter was riding his gray mare home one stormy night after some heavy toping when, as lightning blazed across the heavens, he espied a bevy of witches dancing in a churchyard. Most of the witches were ugly and old. However, one, provocatively dressed in a cutty sark —Scottish dialect for "short chemise"—was young, lovely and extraordinarily graceful.

Tam reined in his mare and paused to watch the beautiful witch as she danced. Overcome with admiration, he suddenly cried out: "Weel done, Cutty Sark!" Instantly the lightning ceased and the churchyard was blotted out by darkness. Tam, terrified, spurred his horse and raced homeward, with the witches in close pursuit. For a moment it appeared that he was done for; the lissome witch came close enough to seize his horse by the tail. But the horse pulled free, leaving its tail in the witch's hand, and Tam rode to safety across the bridge that spanned the River Doon; the witches, it seems, could not cross water.

No one knows precisely what aspect of this tale prompted Jock Willis, a Scotsman and one of the leading shippers of 19th Century London, to choose the name *Cutty Sark* for the tea clipper he commissioned in 1869. Willis wanted a vessel that would be the fastest in the world, and perhaps he hoped to impart to his ship the witch's speed. For a time he must have suspected that he had instead endowed his ship with a dark enchantment: Her career at sea was shadowed by ill fortune and even tragedy for many years. Ultimately, however, the *Cutty Sark* displayed a happier likeness to her namesake, exerting an almost irresistible claim on the affections of all those who knew her either firsthand or by reputation. No other clipper ship won such renown, and she brought the age of sail to its glorious zenith.

Like the lass in the Scottish tale, the *Cutty Sark* was somewhat improbable from the start. In 1869, when she was a-building, merchants who dealt in foreign goods were turning more and more to steamships to transport their cargoes. About the only ports then beyond the reach of steamships were those of Australia and the Far East—too distant for steamers to reach on the supply of coal they could carry from Europe. However, shippers were about to get a new gateway to the Orient: The Suez Canal was being dug to connect the Mediterranean with the Red Sea. Indeed, Empress Eugénie of France would preside at the opening of the canal less than a week before the *Cutty Sark* was launched. A narrow, shoal-strewn passage of no use to sailing vessels, the canal promised to

*The archrivals Cutty Sark (right) and Thermopylae battle for an early lead during their 1872 race from China to England. This first meeting capped two years of intense competition, during which the Thermopylae had bested the Cutty Sark's Shanghai-to-London time by five days in 1870 and two days in 1871.*

make the tea trade a viable proposition for steamers by eliminating the circuitous run around the Cape of Good Hope; it would shorten the distance between the British Isles and China by almost 4,000 miles.

Still, not all shipping companies were ready to abandon their graceful sailing vessels for smoke-belching steamers. Some shippers were certain that human beings could not withstand the grim work of stoking steam engines in the suffocating heat of the Red Sea. Others predicted that the steamships themselves would give out under the strain of lengthy voyages. And partisans of sailing ships could cite the opinion of many tea connoisseurs that tea transported in iron hulls took on unsavory scents. For all these reasons, a dozen clipper ships were launched in the year 1869.

No shipowner was more enamored of sail than Jock Willis, an eccentric known variously as "Captain John," "Old Jock" or—in reference to the pale beaver topper he invariably wore about the London waterfront—"Old White Hat." Sent to sea as a boy, he had eventually worked his way up to captain and voyaged to the far corners of the world. When

he took over his father's firm of John Willis & Son, he had firsthand knowledge of ships and a ready grasp of human nature.

He was meticulous in every phase of the business. No Willis ship sailed without Jock's coming down from his office on Leadenhall Street to preside over the occasion. As the towline tautened to draw the ship out of the harbor, the apprentices lined the rail and called out, "Good-by, sir!" His long white beard waving in the breeze, Old Jock raised his topper and replied, "Good-by, my lads!" Another Willis ship was officially under way—and another bond had been forged between the shipowner and the men who sailed his vessels.

Jock Willis had a strong competitive streak. In 1868, when a rival British shipowner, George Thompson, launched the clipper *Thermopylae* and asserted she would be the fastest sailing ship afloat, Willis bridled. But the *Thermopylae* was true to her billing. Her first passage home from China took only 91 days. Atop her mainmast she proudly wore a weather vane in the form of a gilded rooster, a symbol of her position as cock of the walk. That was a challenge Willis could not resist.

*In a signed pencil drawing by the Cutty Sark's designer, Hercules Linton, the vessel's hull rests half-completed on the stocks (left of center) at Scott & Linton's shipyard in Dumbarton, Scotland. Having won the construction assignment with an unrealistically low bid, the fledgling firm went broke in midventure, and Scott & Linton's creditors hired another shipbuilding company to finish the historic clipper.*

Forthwith, he ordered a new clipper built for his own fleet. She was to be the *Cutty Sark*.

For his new ship Jock Willis turned to a new designer—but to a tried and true design. The flagship of his fleet, and until now his favorite sailer, was the *Tweed*, a 1,745-ton, frigate-like merchant vessel that he had bought as a paddle steamer from another firm because he liked her lines and because she was built of Malabar teak, a handsome, rot-resistant wood to which he was especially partial. He promptly had her converted to sail. The rebuilt *Tweed* proved a fast, easily handled sailer, and Willis thought her strengths could be adapted to the clipper design to produce a ship without peer.

The designer he chose was a 33-year-old shipbuilder named Hercules Linton, who had recently formed a partnership with 24-year-old William Scott in Dumbarton, Scotland. The choice was a gamble, for they had launched only one vessel together. But Linton had learned his craft in the famous Aberdeen yard of Hall, builder of the *Stornoway* and the *Chrysolite*, the first British ships to rival the American clippers. Willis' keen eye told him their work was good, and his sharp business sense enabled him to drive a hard bargain. Because the two eager young men could not resist the chance to build a ship for a man of Willis' stature, they agreed to a construction price of £17 per ton—£2 per ton less than the Hall yard got for a typical clipper ship.

With the deal arranged, Willis gave Linton a tour of the *Tweed* in dry dock. Linton, who had a mind of his own, took inspiration from the *Tweed*, but he did not copy her blindly. He found the *Tweed's* stern too barrel-shaped for his liking, and so he gave the *Cutty Sark* a squarer stern frame and bilge (some early critics said this feature made her look like a clumsy cart horse instead of a thoroughbred racer, but it enabled her to carry extra sail). Linton also knew the virtues of his native Firth of Forth fishing boats, which were renowned throughout the British Isles for their speed and seaworthiness, and so he fashioned the *Cutty Sark* with a bottom like theirs, considerably squarer than that of a typical clipper ship of the day. The product of this mixed lineage was an altogether original vessel.

In length the *Cutty Sark* measured 212.5 feet—half a foot longer than the *Thermopylae*, 15 feet longer than the *Ariel*. More heavily sparred than any other tea clipper, she could carry as much sail as a 1,500-ton frigate. When dressed in her full suit of sails, she spread three quarters of an acre of canvas. All that sail, manipulated with 10 miles of lines, could provide a driving force equivalent to 3,000 horsepower.

Willis had already decided to award the command of the *Cutty Sark* to George Moodie, who had served as first mate of the *Tweed*. He therefore sent Moodie up to Dumbarton to supervise her construction. Moodie was as much a stickler for perfection as Willis himself. Nothing but perfect timbers would do for the *Cutty Sark's* hull; nothing but perfect planks would do for her decks—and the main deck had to be all in teak. Predictably, her finishing touches were elegant. A line made of gold leaf ran along the sides of her black-painted hull at the level of the main deck. Gold leaf was also used for the ship's name and the words "Port of London" that emblazoned the stern in raised letters encircled in laurel

OWNER JOCK WILLIS

CAPTAIN GEORGE MOODIE

*After collaborating in the creation of the clipper Cutty Sark, each of these four Scotsmen ventured into new fields. Owner Jock Willis joined the board of a company that owned docks. Designer Hercules Linton became assistant manager of a shipyard that built steamers. Chief draftsman John Rennie, who drew up the plans for the Cutty Sark, worked as a naval architect in China, where he was appointed a mandarin for his services. Willis' overseer of work on the clipper, Captain George Moodie, finally quit the sea and took up the study of meteorology.*

DESIGNER HERCULES LINTON

CHIEF DRAFTSMAN JOHN RENNIE

Tam o'Shanter, above, flees on horseback from a comely witch wearing a cutty sark—Scottish dialect for "short chemise." In designer Hercules Linton's original drawing for the clipper Cutty Sark's figurehead (left), the witch clutches a remnant of the horse's tail. The actual figurehead lacked the trophy, but the ship's crew often stuffed a hank of rope in the witch's outstretched hand.

wreaths. A Junoesque figurehead representing the witch in the short chemise graced the bow.

The *Cutty Sark* was launched on November 22, 1869. Twelve weeks later she sailed from London for China—the first test of what she could do at sea. Throughout the passage, Captain Moodie was preoccupied with delicate tuning of the sails and rigging. On days when he hit the right combination, the *Cutty Sark* responded and made good runs: 343 miles in one 24-hour period, 360 miles in another (averaging a spirited 14½ knots and 15 knots, respectively). But on days when the tuning went amiss, the *Cutty Sark* balked and slowed down to a maddening crawl. In the end she took 104 days to reach Shanghai—not a bad performance, but not an outstanding one either. "I was on board her in China at the end of her maiden run," one seaman later recalled, "and, the same as a good many there, did not know whether I quite liked her or not. However," he added, "we were all bad prophets."

Just then Moodie had a more pressing problem than the *Cutty Sark's* popularity, and that was the matter of filling her hold with tea. About a dozen steamers that were taking advantage of the new Suez Canal had already snapped up the lion's share of the first tea harvest. After a month's wait for a later crop, Captain Moodie did manage to negotiate a cargo of 1,305,812 pounds of tea for the *Cutty Sark*—but only at the disappointing rate of 3 pounds 10 shillings per 50 cubic feet, about half what clippers had commanded before the canal opened.

There remained the challenge of testing her speed on the run home against that of the *Thermopylae*. The race was against the clock, for the two ships did not depart together. The *Cutty Sark* set out on June 25 and reached London after 110 days. The *Thermopylae*, sailing separately a month later—and with better winds—made the trip in 105 days.

The *Cutty Sark's* second voyage to China the following year was made in an equally undistinguished 108 days. She did beat the *Ariel* home by a week, but she was still outrun by the *Thermopylae*, which made the trip in 106 days. Again, however, the *Thermopylae* had better weather, and so the hopes of Willis, Moodie and the crew remained high.

On her third voyage, in 1872, the *Cutty Sark* got the long-awaited chance to race the *Thermopylae* home in the same weather and under the same conditions. She and the *Thermopylae* both left the mouth of the Shanghai River on June 18, 1872. Both were held up for three days by fog. When the weather cleared, they sped down the China Sea, exchanging the lead several times over the next four weeks. At 2 p.m. on July 25, the lookout perched high in the *Cutty Sark's* crosstrees saw the *Thermopylae* almost three miles ahead. At about that point the rivals lost sight of each other. The wind freshened and the *Cutty Sark* surged forward, logging runs of 340, 327 and 320 miles during one three-day period. At the end of two weeks she was—although Moodie did not realize it at the time—400 miles ahead.

Then on August 9, when the *Cutty Sark* had reached the Indian Ocean, a heavy gale blew up. For six days the wind mauled the clipper and, in a final savage blow on August 15, tore off her rudder, which, having heavy iron fittings, plunged straight to the bottom of the ocean.

Making repairs at sea was a familiar enough challenge to sailors of the day; every sailing vessel carried spare spars and sails, and the mending of the rigging was all in a day's work. But the loss of a rudder was uncommon. Faced with the loss of so vital a part of the ship, most captains would have limped as best they could to a port where ship-building expertise was available. One man aboard the *Cutty Sark* was in favor of Moodie's doing just that. He was Robert Willis, brother of the owner, and he peremptorily commanded Captain Moodie to put in to the nearest South African port. The two men swore at each other; then Moodie, far from yielding to his cantankerous passenger, hove to and addressed himself instead to the demands of his stricken ship.

He was lucky in finding a small model of the *Cutty Sark* on board; it enabled him to calculate the measurements for a new rudder. He directed the carpenter to fashion a rudder by sawing heavy planks out of spare spars. To join them together, the blacksmith had to forge iron fittings from the ship's awning stanchions.

*Dignitaries gather to watch French Empress Eugénie, inside the large pavilion at center, open the Suez Canal on November 17, 1869. In the two smaller tents, Catholics and Muslims "this once joined to pray for a single object," reported a London newspaper. The event marked the end of clipper hegemony in the tea trade, as steam vessels began using the canal route to China.*

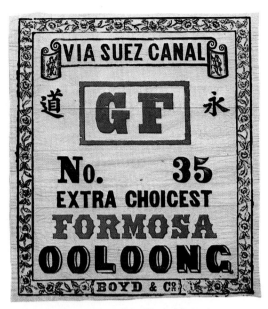

The words "via Suez Canal" on this tea label were meant to inform the buyer that the product was weeks fresher than if it had come from China by the much longer route by sail around the Cape of Good Hope. Though some connoisseurs thought the steamers' iron hulls caused tea to deteriorate, steamer-carried tea sold well.

The work went on for four days as the *Cutty Sark* bounced and lurched on the rough sea. One great wave washed over the deck, knocking down the forge and with it the blacksmith and an apprentice—Captain Moodie's young son Alexander, who was working the bellows. The blacksmith's beard was singed by a red-hot iron bar that had been dislodged, and Alexander's chest was to bear the scars of flying hot coals for the rest of his life. Undeterred by such setbacks, the entire ship's company labored on—all except Robert Willis, who continued to strut about the poop, muttering curses at the captain and his benighted undertaking.

At last the *Cutty Sark* was fitted with her jury rudder and ready to hobble around the Cape of Good Hope and on to London, where she arrived on October 18, 122 days after leaving her pilot in Shanghai. Although the *Thermopylae* had docked a week earlier, the *Cutty Sark* had made an 8,000-mile passage with makeshift steering gear in an incredible 60 days—not much longer than an ordinary sailing vessel might take when fully fit. Some people thought that the race itself paled by comparison with Moodie's feat of seamanship in getting the jury rudder fashioned and affixed in stormy waters. By any reckoning, the *Cutty Sark* was a national heroine overnight.

The abuse the captain had taken from Robert Willis had put Moodie in a huff, and he resigned his command after the voyage. Old Jock tried every means of persuasion to induce him to stay, even promising that his brother would never go to sea again. But Moodie was adamant and found himself another berth as captain of a steamship belonging to a Glasgow firm, leaving Old Jock to fume that Moodie was pigheaded.

Old Jock had more reasons than one to regret losing his crack captain. More and more captains were succumbing to the seductions of steam vessels, with their ever-speedier passages and consequently rising rates of pay. Good masters were becoming hard to find, and during the next 10 years Willis and his precious *Cutty Sark* would suffer from a run of captains who ranged from timid to terrible.

The first was Francis William Moore, who had recently served as superintendent of the Willis shipyards. At the age of 50, Moore was beyond driving a ship hard; moreover, his tenure as superintendent had left him with an aversion to causing wear and tear on a ship. Therefore he refused to allow the *Cutty Sark* sufficient sail for her sturdy hull to make the most of good winds. Under Moore's reluctant hand, the *Cutty Sark* stubbornly took 110 days to make the passage from England to Shanghai, and another 117 to return.

Willis immediately replaced Moore with Captain William Edward Tiptaft, who had been commanding lesser vessels in the company's fleet. The *Cutty Sark* still made no long-distance records and won no races. But already she was demonstrating that she could do better in stiff winds than in light ones. One mariner, recalling a voyage under Tiptaft's command, was to write later that "it got to be quite a common saying then: 'Fifteen knots and two apprentices,' as it took two to hold the reel" when her speed was being measured by running a log line off a spool. In the hands of a sure sailor, the clipper clearly could run fast enough. But Tiptaft died of a heart attack in Shanghai in 1878, and Willis resumed his search for the right master for the *Cutty Sark*. ⚓

# A bonny synthesis of wood, iron and canvas

With her gleaming brass fittings, delicately carved scrollwork and polished teak handrails, the *Cutty Sark* looked more like a millionaire's yacht than a toiling merchantman. But underneath her elegant exterior, the sleek clipper was a sturdy work horse of a ship— one of the most powerful sailing machines ever built.

Launched in 1869, the *Cutty Sark* boasted an iron-ribbed, wood-planked hull that proved both exceptionally strong and very fast. With her two immense holds crammed with a full cargo of 1.3 million pounds of tea, the clipper could blast through the seas at a top speed of 17½ knots, driven by a towering three-masted rig of square sails capable of generating more than 3,000 horsepower from the wind.

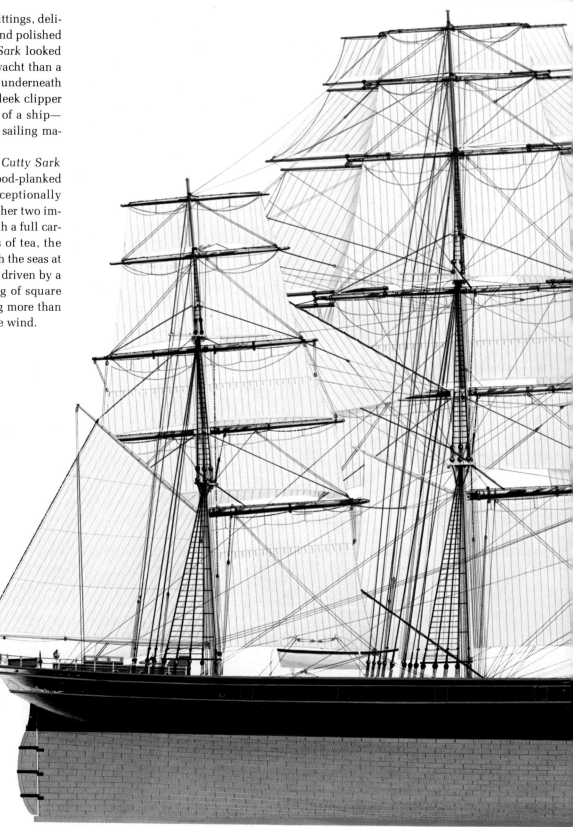

With her mainmast rising 145.9
feet above her deck and her main yard
extending 78 feet from tip to tip, the
Cutty Sark carried more sail for her size
than any other clipper ship ever built.
When all her studding sails were set, she
flung 32,000 square feet of canvas
before the wind. These views show her as
originally rigged, before alterations
in 1880 reduced the height of her masts
and the amount of sail she carried.

The *Cutty Sark's* unusual half-wood, half-iron hull was a memorable example of necessity mothering invention. Most earlier British clippers, and all their American forerunners, had been built of wood. For strength and ease of cutting and shaping, hardwood was unsurpassed as a shipbuilding material. But by the 1860s, England's oak forests were seriously depleted, and teak had become so expensive that orders for wooden clippers almost ceased.

Iron cost less than wood and, pound for pound, was stronger. However, one serious drawback prevented its use on China clippers: On a long voyage through warm seas, iron hulls became heavily fouled with barnacles, adding weeks to a trip. Wooden planking could be covered with copper sheets to prevent barnacle growth. But copper could not be affixed to an iron hull be-cause an electrochemical reaction that took place between the two metals in sea water would corrode and destroy the iron. Not until the 1870s, with the perfection of copper-based antifouling paints, could iron-hulled ships travel the clippers' warm-water routes.

For clippers of the 1860s, the answer was a hull that limited the use of iron to the internal skeleton. The 963-ton *Cutty Sark* was constructed of six-

1. STEERING GEARS
2. CAPTAIN'S STATEROOM
3. SKYLIGHT
4. SALOON
5. OFFICERS' QUARTERS
6. DIAGONAL TIE PLATE
7. STRINGER PLATE
8. KEEL
9. RIB
10. COPPER SHEATHING
11. WOOD PLANKING
12. ANGLE PLATE
13. DECK BEAM
14. BOOBY HATCH
15. FIRE BUCKET
16. LIFEBOAT DAVIT
17. LIFEBOAT
18. JOLLY BOAT
19. STUDDING-SAIL SPAR
20. APPRENTICES' BUNKS
21. BOSUN'S CABIN
22. DECK FLUSH PORT
23. BILGE PUMP
24. MAIN HATCH

inch-thick planks of teak rising from a 15-by-17-inch keel of solid rock elm. This exterior sheathing was double-bolted to iron ribs that were reinforced by diagonal tie plates and horizontal stringer plates. More iron beams, angle plates and iron pillars supported the cargo deck and the main deck.

All the *Cutty Sark*'s ironwork was top quality, capable of bearing a stress of 20 tons per square inch. Only the finest grade of seasoned and knot-free wood was chosen for planking. The seams between rows of planks were calked with the best brown oakum, and each plank end was fitted with an iron cap to seal it from the water. The bottom of the vessel was covered with sheets of antifouling copper that were tacked over a coating of white lead and tallow. In the hull, all inaccessible cavities in the bow and stern were filled with cement in order to prevent rot.

Before she was launched, the *Cutty Sark* was examined by the surveyors from Lloyd's Register, who rated her 16A1, which meant that she had the highest insurance classification, and that it was guaranteed for 16 years. In fact, the *Cutty Sark* was so strongly built that she roamed the oceans of the world for more than 50 grueling years without ever suffering a major leak.

| | |
|---|---|
| 25. KEELSON | 33. GIG |
| 26. HOLD | 34. DECK WINCH |
| 27. LOWER DECK | 35. FORWARD HATCH |
| 28. TEA CHEST | 36. WATER CLOSET |
| 29. IRON PILLAR | 37. PIGPEN |
| 30. GALLEY | 38. PAINT LOCKER |
| 31. CARPENTER'S SHOP | 39. ADDITIONAL CREW QUARTERS |
| 32. CREW QUARTERS | 40. CEMENT FILLING |

John Batchelor

*Hard-driving James Smith Wallace was the fourth captain of the Cutty Sark but the first to demonstrate her great speed. Immediately after taking the helm in 1878, Wallace made a brilliant 16-day run between Shanghai and the Sunda Strait, averaging more than 15 knots.*

After Tiptaft's death, the next man to take command of the *Cutty Sark* was James Smith Wallace, who had been first mate under Tiptaft. Wallace turned out to be a first-rate seaman who was finely attuned to the intricacies of sail; for three years he drove the *Cutty Sark* hard and well. He was also a jovial man whose crew liked him; he joked with everyone and displayed inexhaustible patience in teaching apprentices their craft. But Wallace lacked decisiveness and had difficulty enforcing discipline. Under him the *Cutty Sark* suffered her first tragedy.

In the spring of 1880, Jock Willis heard that the United States Navy was offering prime freight rates for speedy delivery of coal to the steamships it had stationed in the Pacific. Coal had none of the glamor of tea; besides being a filthy and unpleasant cargo, it was a highly flammable one. But it paid well, and such was the grip of steamers on the tea market that the *Cutty Sark* had been unable to get a tea cargo on her last trip to China. So Jock Willis—reluctantly concluding that he would have to give up his quest for preeminence in tea races—decided to alter the *Cutty Sark*, tailoring her for trade in which swiftness was not paramount. In March 1880 he had nine feet six inches cut off her lower masts and seven feet off the lower yards, and he shortened her upper masts and yards in proportion, thinking that the resulting reduction in sail area would make her easier to operate and a more reliable, if somewhat slower, sailer. (In fact, the surgery turned out to be just what she needed to perform at her very best.) Two months later, with Captain Wallace still in command, Willis sent the *Cutty Sark* off to Penarth, Wales, to fill her hold with coal. From there she set sail for Yokohama, Japan.

Captain Wallace had a doubtful complement of officers this time. The first mate, who was listed in the ship's articles as Sidney Smith, may have been traveling under an alias. If so, he had good reason for concealing his identity; he proved to be a ruthless bucko mate. The second mate was not a bad fellow at heart, but he was so nearsighted that he could not see to the top of the rigging; the amiable Wallace stood watch with him to help him out. The third mate was a former apprentice who had failed his examination for second mate.

The crewmen proved to be no more promising than the officers. Among them was a chronic doomsayer whom the apprentices nicknamed the Flying Dutchman, an allusion to the legendary ship that was fated to wander interminably, ever in search of a welcoming port. When Wallace made the mistake of setting sail from Penarth on a Friday—a day traditionally held by sailors everywhere to be bad luck—he thoughtlessly gave the Flying Dutchman cause for muttering gloomy prophecies into the ears of a superstitious crew. Another crew member was a black man named John Francis, who seemed to have a knack for doing everything wrong. His clumsiness brought repeated tongue-lashings from the first mate.

Trouble came as the *Cutty Sark* was crossing the Indian Ocean and heading for Anyer Lor on the Sunda Strait, where she was to put in to receive instructions from Willis in London. Captain Wallace ordered a slight shift of course. "Slack away the tack," Smith shouted. The man at the bow, who should have responded by loosening a foresail sheet, was John Francis. Perhaps he was napping; perhaps he did not hear well; perhaps he was in a bad mood and deliberately chose to disobey. In any event, nothing happened, and the mate rushed forward in a rage, yelling obscenities.

He reached the bow to find Francis clutching a capstan bar. The two men wrestled for a moment. Smith wrenched the heavy wooden bar away, gave it a powerful swing and brought it thudding down on Francis' skull. Francis dropped to the deck. Another seaman slackened the sheet, the clipper fell off on her new course, and Francis' unconscious body was carried to his bunk. He died there three days later.

The crew had no love for Francis. But the violence of the deed—and their own ill treatment at the hands of the mate—was enough to put them on the side of the hapless victim. Captain Wallace had no sooner read a funeral service and buried Francis at sea than the crew turned sullen to an alarming degree. Wallace confined Smith below, and took over the mate's duties himself.

Throughout this disturbance the *Cutty Sark* had made a swift passage from Wales to the Sunda Strait, reaching Anyer Lor in 72 days, earlier than expected. Consequently, there was not yet a telegram giving instructions from Willis. While waiting for his employer's message, Wallace took steps to deal with the troubles on his ship—and, in so doing, he made a fatal mistake.

Lying at anchor in the roadstead, not far from the *Cutty Sark*, was the American merchantman *Colorado*. Wallace called on the *Colorado's* captain and (presumably withholding intelligence of the killing) asked if his fellow captain could use another mate. The American said yes. Before making the transfer, Wallace arranged to have a few Indonesian bumboats come alongside the *Cutty Sark's* starboard rail, and handed out some spending money to his crew. While the men were absorbed in haggling with the islanders over such local exotica as pineapples, Java sparrows and parakeets, Wallace allowed Smith to slip over the port side into a small boat, which whisked him away.

Captain Wallace never explained what led him to conspire with his mate as he did. Perhaps he felt that Smith had killed the surly seaman in self-defense. If so, he should have taken Smith ashore and had him stand trial. By helping Smith to escape, Wallace broke the law. In addition, he put his crew in a fury. When a telegram finally arrived from Jock Willis bringing orders to proceed to Yokohama, the crewmen announced—with the Flying Dutchman as their spokesman—that they would neither raise anchor nor tend sail.

Making do with his officers and apprentices, Wallace took the *Cutty Sark* into the Java Sea—and a maddening calm. For three days the clipper slatted in the swells, rolling aimlessly. The crew sulked in the forecastle. The Flying Dutchman added to their bad temper by making dire predictions that worse was yet to come. Captain Wallace paced the quarter-deck day and night. He seemed never to sleep or even to nap. His joviality was gone. Clearly he was in anguish.

In the early hours of the fourth day at sea, Wallace could stand the pressure no longer. At 4 a.m., when the watch was changing, he walked to the helm and told the helmsman to check his course. As the man

# The dismal fates of once-proud vessels

Although the *Cutty Sark* seemed to last forever, the life of most clippers was downright ephemeral. Nearly one quarter of the sleek racers came to grief before they were 10 years old. Most of them, including many that were in the China trade, were pounded to pieces on reefs or rocky lee shores. The *Oriental* struck a rock and sank in 1854 while she was en route down the treacherous Min River from Foochow, the speedy *Flying Fish* was condemned after grounding at the mouth of the Min in 1858, and the *Taeping* foundered on a China Sea reef in 1871.

Others vanished at sea with all hands, presumably victims of storms. These included the pioneering clipper *Rainbow* in 1848, the *Houqua* in 1864 and the tea racer *Ariel* in 1872. And fire, the bane of all wooden ships, consumed its share of clippers. The *Hornet (below)* caught fire when a seaman spilled varnish near a lantern, and the *John Gilpin* burned while carrying a cargo of whale oil.

As steamships took over the most lucrative trades, several clippers became ordinary tramp freighters, hauling lumber, grain, coal and other bulk goods. After years of tramping, the *Great Republic* sank off Bermuda in 1872. The *Flying Cloud* carried timber until 1874, when she piled up on the Newfoundland coast. The *Wild Pigeon*, which had been re-rigged as a bark, finally sank in the North Atlantic in 1892.

A few old clippers entered the despised African slave trade. Others carried loads of stinking guano from the Chincha Islands in the Pacific. And many suffered the ultimate humiliation of a sailing vessel: They were dismasted and used as coaling barges for steamships.

The pioneers of the clipper era generally fared better than their ships. Captain Nat Palmer, who whittled the first model of the *Houqua*, retired to Connecticut and helped found the New York Yacht Club. Captain Josiah Creesy of the *Flying Cloud* served with the Union Navy during the Civil War, and afterward retired and lived in Salem, Massachusetts, with his wife. Ocean pathfinder Matthew Fontaine Maury planned the route of the first transatlantic telegraph cable before the War, then, being a native Southerner developed electrically detonated mines for the Confederacy.

The sudden demise of the clippers nearly bankrupted master shipbuilder Donald McKay, but he rebounded to construct Union ironclads and commercial steamships before he retired in 1877. And John Griffiths, who designed the *Rainbow* in 1843, turned his talents to steamship design—but he went to his grave in 1882 insisting that wooden hulls were better than steel.

*Sheets of flame roar from the sinking clipper* Hornet *while a boatload of her seamen begin to jury-rig a mast.*

leaned over to study the dimly lit binnacle, Wallace climbed onto the taffrail and dropped overboard.

At the sound of the splash, the helmsman called out and tossed two life preservers over the stern. The crewmen forgot their grudge and rushed to lower a boat to aid their captain, but to no avail. In the darkness they saw nothing but the two life rings floating on the water—and the fins of several sharks. Captain Wallace had vanished.

It was a contrite crew that brought the *Cutty Sark* back to Anyer Lor. Jock Willis, informed by cable of Wallace's fate, was at a loss to understand events taking place half a world away, since he had not been told of the death of Francis or the escape of the mate. All he could do was ask the second mate to take command—only to have the mate protest that he was incompetent to do so. Finally Willis arranged for a Dutch pilot to go aboard and navigate the ship to Singapore.

At Singapore most of the crew deserted—among them the Flying Dutchman, who vowed to devote the rest of his life to pursuing Smith until he was brought to justice. Two years later Smith, then going under the alias of Anderson, was recognized in London by one of the men who had sailed with him on the *Cutty Sark*—perhaps the Flying Dutchman, although the man's identity is not known. The former mate was taken into custody, brought to trial, convicted of manslaughter and sentenced to seven years' hard labor.

Meanwhile, Willis faced the problem of finding another captain for the *Cutty Sark* in Singapore. Since his nearest clipper was the *Hallowe'en* in Hong Kong, he cabled her captain, Robert Warrender Fowler, to ask him if the *Hallowe'en's* first mate, William H. Bruce, would be capable of assuming command of the *Cutty Sark*. It happened that Fowler despised Bruce. Jumping at the unexpected chance to be rid of him, Fowler replied to Willis in one word: "Yes." Bruce immediately took passage to Singapore—and the *Cutty Sark* acquired the most nefarious captain of her lifetime.

Captain Fowler's abhorrence of his first mate was completely understandable. Bruce, a fat little man with protruding eyes and a high-pitched tenor voice, was a split personality—a Bible-thumping evangelist and a drunken sot by turns. With him as her captain, the *Cutty Sark* embarked on a three-year nightmare that would not be relieved by a single good passage.

Willis ordered Bruce to proceed in ballast to Calcutta, and there find another cargo. The passage from Singapore to Calcutta took 42 days, half again as long as it should have, because Bruce was drunk much of the time and kept shortening sail for no apparent reason.

After the *Cutty Sark* finally reached Calcutta, she lay at anchor in the Hooghly River while Captain Bruce, unable to find a cargo, spent his time preaching fire and brimstone at a local church. The crew was paid off. At length the gullible congregation of English colonists presented Bruce with a gold watch for his inspirational services, and he found a cargo of Indian tea. With that cargo he achieved his one distinction—bringing the first cargo of Indian tea to Australia, where it was to find a vigorous market in the growing colony.

On this passage, however, the *Cutty Sark* suffered a bitter humiliation:

She floundered off the Australian coast while Bruce needlessly checked and rechecked his bearings, and a much slower ship that had left Calcutta a week later romped past her into Melbourne.

From then on, one calamity followed another. From Melbourne the *Cutty Sark* doubled back to Sydney to fetch a load of coal for Shanghai. She no sooner reached Shanghai than an outbreak of cholera killed two members of her crew and left most of the rest so weak that they could hardly work the ship when she took off on the next leg, a passage to the Philippines for a cargo of jute to go to New York. In the Sunda Strait she almost ran aground because Captain Bruce was drunk and paying no attention to the helm. In the Indian Ocean a seaman fell to his death from the rigging. In the South Atlantic the crew had to be put on half rations because Bruce had not stocked enough provisions for the voyage. Before she reached her destination the food was gone, and the proud ship was reduced to begging from passing vessels. When the *Cutty Sark* reached New York Harbor on April 10, 1882, the men were half-starved and altogether disgruntled, and the vessel herself was a sorry sight, with tattered sails, frayed rigging, and a rusted windlass.

*Whiling away the days of waiting for a cargo of wool, officers and apprentices gather with female guests for a group portrait aboard the Cutty Sark at Sydney in 1887. Captain Richard Woodget, wearing the tam-o'-shanter that became his trademark, is leaning on the poop rail (back row, third from right).*

At long last, however, relief was in store for the sadly used clipper. From his agent in New York, Old Jock had learned of the *Cutty Sark's* miserable state. Luckily, another Willis vessel, the *Blackadder,* was in New York with an able commander aboard. He was Captain Frederick Moore (no relation to the F. W. Moore who had succeeded Captain Moodie aboard the *Cutty Sark* in 1872), and Willis transferred him and his officers to the *Cutty Sark.* Moore, a tall, bearded, reticent man, took his new charge to India for redwood, brown sugar and dyes, and then to London. She arrived in her home port on June 2, 1883, her first appearance there since May 6, 1880.

Moore's career aboard the *Cutty Sark* was a brief one and might not be remembered save for the important fact that it represented a turning point in the *Cutty Sark's* life. Approaching her 15th year—a ripe old age for a clipper—the *Cutty Sark* under this new master proved that her hull was still as sound as on the day of launching and that she still had a promising future.

The *Cutty Sark* had spent eight years carrying tea, and another five years tramping in search of any cargo she could get. By the time Moore took over at her helm, the Suez Canal had been open for more than a decade, and steamers had gained total control of the China trade. The clippers had necessarily been diverted to other trades that lay along routes where coaling stations had not yet been opened. Some clippers entered exclusively into the jute and sugar traffic of the Philippines; others specialized in commerce with India. Some did as the *Cutty Sark* had done, tramping from port to port.

Meanwhile, a boom in the Australian wool trade had created a new market for clipper service. Australia, which still lay beyond practical reach of steamers, was exporting more than a million tons of wool annually to the textile factories of England. Speedy delivery of wool had become nearly as important and as lucrative as quick delivery of fresh tea had been three decades before. The London exchange auctioned wool only from January through March. If a wool merchant missed the first auctions, he had to pay high warehouse prices to hold the wool for the next time around. Given the possibility of such a financial setback, clipper delivery seemed a wise investment.

Under Captain Moore, the *Cutty Sark* set off from London for a wool cargo in July 1883. She came romping home from Australia in an astonishing 82 days, 25 days faster than her nearest competitors. The following year she lowered her time to 80 days. The *Thermopylae,* which also had entered into the wool trade, managed to tie this time, but the *Cutty Sark* had proved that she was the equal of her old rival.

In the spring of 1885, Willis transferred Moore to another ship (his onetime favorite, the *Tweed*) and put aboard the *Cutty Sark* a 40-year-old Norfolk man named Richard Woodget. He would sail her into history.

Captain Woodget's father was a farmer, but Richard himself had demonstrated both an independent spirit and a bent for seamanship at an early age. As a boy, he stole a rudderless sailing dinghy, spent an afternoon teaching himself not only how to sail but how to steer by the sail alone, without a rudder, and returned the boat to its mooring before the loss was discovered. At 16 he went to sea as an apprentice, and during the next 20 years he worked his way up through the ranks to captain. By the time he earned his first command, he had become an expert at sailmaking, rigging and navigation. He had also established a reputation for eccentricity. In a day when most captains sported pot hats—stiff-crowned headgear such as bowlers—Woodget wore a cap at a rakish angle. Appropriately for the prospective master of the *Cutty Sark*, it was a tam-o'-shanter.

All those qualities, combined with his intrepid nerve and iron will, made him the perfect match for the *Cutty Sark*. In 1885 he was new to the Willis firm, but Jock Willis was quick to note his talents. As soon as Woodget returned from his first voyage, Willis took him down to the East India Dock. Pointing to the *Cutty Sark*, he said: "Captain Woodget, there is your ship. All you have to do is drive her."

Woodget, who liked to boast, "Give me two boys and I'll rig a ship," made the *Cutty Sark's* neglected rigging his first concern. He began at once to tromp the deck, inspecting every line and fitting. Within days he had replaced all her outworn hempen braces and headsail sheets with supple wire. He put new barrel winches at the main rail for the heavy work of handling the foresail and mainsheets and tacks. Men installing the new rigging were surprised to find Captain Woodget himself alongside them on the footropes; he climbed aloft to supervise the work on every yard, to the top of every mast.

It took several months to get the *Cutty Sark* in the shape that Woodget wanted, and Willis did not stint on funds. On April 1, 1885, newly rigged, calked and painted from stem to stern, she was ready. Woodget pulled his tam-o'-shanter down tight on his head at 2 p.m. and ordered the lines cast off. Slowly the gleaming ship edged away from the East India Dock, bound for Australia—and for the feats of speed that had always seemed within her power.

Having personally examined every inch of the clipper's new rigging, Woodget knew exactly what the old sailer could do. So when the *Cutty Sark*, after making an easy run down the Atlantic, rounded the Cape of Good Hope and picked up a strong northeasterly, he confidently piled on a full suit of sails. For three days, with everything drawing, the *Cutty Sark* sped across the Indian Ocean at a pace that sometimes approached 16 knots.

Woodget was a hard driver but a prudent one, and the crew delighted in watching him at work. "He fairly reveled in it," one of his officers wrote later. "With one side of his moustache jammed into his mouth, and hanging on to the weather rigging, I can see him now, his sturdy figure in yellow oilskins and long leather sea boots, watching aloft and hanging on till the last minute."

Woodget drove the men as he drove the ship, refusing to be deflected

*Docked at Sydney's busy Circular Quay, the Cutty Sark— her 60-foot jib boom hauled aboard to avoid interfering with passing traffic—loads bales of wool arriving by horse- drawn wagon. Between 1885 and 1894, the clipper lugged some 46,000 bales—weighing a grand total of 18.6 million pounds—from Australia to ports in England and Belgium.*

from his purpose, and demanding complete obedience in all things and at all times—even when he was conducting church services on deck. On one Sunday, when a breaking wave that spilled over the deck nearly washed the men off their knees and a crewman looked imploringly up at the captain, Woodget bellowed, "Close your damned eyes, Bill Jones, and let me finish this prayer!"

Such steadfast determination served him well in all kinds of weather. When strong winds dropped off and were succeeded by contrary breezes and calms, Woodget still seemed to be able to keep the *Cutty Sark* moving. She made the 15,000-mile run to Sydney in 78 days.

Among the clipper-ship captains and crews in the wool trade, rivalry ran high, just as it had during the tea races two and three decades before. Each ship vied for the honor of being first home to London, and each had her champions among local bettors in the Sydney pubs. Not surprisingly, the two clippers that the odds favored in 1885 were the *Cutty Sark* and the *Thermopylae*.

The *Thermopylae* came into the harbor in August, a few weeks after the *Cutty Sark*. During the weeks spent waiting for the wool to be brought to the quay and loaded, the *Thermopylae* rode to anchor flaunting the gilded cock at her masthead, symbolizing the preeminence she had not yet lost. Watching it flashing in the sunlight one day, Woodget vowed to his third mate, "I'll pull that damned bauble off her." Not since the fateful episode of the jury rudder under Captain Moodie in 1872 had the two vessels raced each other over the same course, at the same time and under the same conditions. Now once again the opportunity to do that had arrived.

Ships on the Australia run sailed east around the world, going outbound around the Cape of Good Hope, and home by way of the fearsome Cape Horn. For Woodget, who had not made the Australia trip before, this was to be a first time around Cape Horn. In Sydney his fellow skippers joked that he would probably get lost. Woodget was known to be far too good a navigator to do that, but the *Cutty Sark* and every other clipper faced problems enough in the huge seas of the roaring forties and the Horn.

All told, nine of the fastest clippers moved out of Sydney Harbor between October 5 and 24, 1885, setting all sails as they began the voyage home. The *Cutty Sark* and the *Thermopylae* left within two days of each other, on the 16th and the 18th, respectively.

Sailing south of New Zealand, the *Cutty Sark* made a nearly straight run for the Horn. She had her first brush with angry seas within a few days—and met the test easily. As each mountain of water rose crackling astern, the *Cutty Sark* responded nimbly; she tucked the onrushing wave under her counter and ran forward on its crest. The high, squared stern that Hercules Linton had designed was ideal for massive following seas such as these.

A more serious trial soon followed. On October 22, a week out of Sydney, the *Cutty Sark* was proceeding eastward before a howling squall of snow and hail. At 11 o'clock that night, a sudden gust sent her reeling. Despite the helmsman's best efforts, she broached to, spinning around so that she came broadside to the wind and the rising sea. Her

# The captain with a camera

One day in 1887, a shipment of peculiarly nonnautical equipment was delivered to the *Cutty Sark* as she lay at London's East India Dock. The delivery included a large supply of photographic plates, the chemicals for processing them, and a mahogany view camera. The *Cutty Sark's* irrepressible captain, Richard Woodget, who had shipboard enthusiasms ranging from breeding prize collies to roller skating, was taking up photography.

The captain approached this latest hobby with characteristic zeal. Most amateurs of the era used small cameras that could be hand-held, but he insisted on having the big, full-plate, professional size, even though it was cumbersome and required tripod support. To develop the 12-by-10-inch glass negatives, he transformed his cabin into a darkroom, using his bathtub as a reservoir for mixing chemicals and washing the developed plates.

Captain Woodget found abundant subject matter within the shipboard world of the *Cutty Sark*. And wherever the opportunity arose, he turned his camera on the grandeur of the world through which she passed.

CAPTAIN RICHARD WOODGET, ABOUT 1900

*In this photograph by Woodget, the Cutty Sark lies at anchor in Sydney Harbor. Although the picture could have been taken from the rigging of another ship, Woodget's camera was so heavy that he probably shot the photograph from a nearby rise on shore.*

In a light breeze, the Cutty Sark moves smoothly through calm, midocean seas. The serene spirit of the photograph belies the difficulty Woodget had taking it: After he had been rowed out to sea in a small, unsteady boat, the captain struggled to focus his camera on the ship while two apprentices tried to keep the legs of the tripod steady.

On the Cutty Sark's poop deck, three collies pose agreeably for their master's camera. Woodget became renowned for the pedigreed dogs he bred aboard the Cutty Sark, many of which became winners in the Australian show ring.

Gathered beside the Cutty's deck winch, three crewmen provide an album entry for their photographer-captain. The man at right is Tony Robson, the Cutty Sark's Chinese-born cook. As an infant, he had been found drifting in a small boat off the coast of China. He grew up on British ships and was, said a mate, "English in every respect but his features."

Seated under the mizzenmast boom, a sailor mends a section of sail as a pensive apprentice looks on. After Woodget's photography sessions, apprentices were summoned to a most nonnautical chore: to serve as darkroom assistants.

*"Passed close by an iceberg, about 300 feet high, and photographed it," Woodget wrote in his log on January 10, 1888, when he took these pictures near Cape Horn. Fascinated by the great formations, he would watch them for hours, leaning on the spanker boom, chin on folded arms; more than once, his beard froze to the boom without his noticing.*

main royal blew out; so did her main upper topsail and even the main- and fore-topgallants. She gave a sickening roll, and the water poured over her lee rail in a torrent. She shuddered, wallowed, then rose with the next sea and lifted her bow, shaking off tons of green water like a rising whale. Away with the water went all the gear on deck, including the port lifeboat.

The trouble, however, was not with the vessel but with the exhausted helmsman—and he recovered within seconds. Battling with all his strength, he brought the *Cutty Sark* back onto her heading and managed to hold her there as the next sea rolled under the stern.

Most captains would have hove to for repairs. Woodget, unwilling to lose a minute, instead sent all hands aloft at once to bend on and reef new topsails. Despite the freezing sheets of rain and stinging sleet, the men worked without letup through the night. And the *Cutty Sark* kept moving forward.

On the next evening at seven came still another danger. The bow lookout suddenly shouted, "Ice on the port bow!" Visibility was poor, and the lookout had failed to notice, until the ship was practically upon it, a monstrous iceberg that was coming perilously close to tearing a fatal gash in the *Cutty Sark's* hull. Woodget quickly ordered a turn to starboard and eluded disaster.

By November 8—only 23 days out of Sydney—the *Cutty Sark* had rounded the Horn. She had shown that she could safely run before the world's biggest waves and strongest winds, survive sail-bursting squalls of snow and hail, and even rise from broaching to. On the next leg of the passage, she would encounter a different set of problems. Sailing north along the east coast of South America, she would have to contend with a series of contrary winds and then go almost head on into northeasterlies. Could she beat against the prevailing winds as well as she had run before the wind?

With Woodget expertly directing the shifting of sail, she could—as almost anyone aboard could have predicted by now. "He gave all his crew complete confidence in him," one of his officers was to recall. "I never remember seeing him anything but calm in dirty weather."

He worked his men so hard they dropped in exhaustion at the end of every watch. But under his inspiration they labored willingly. And as they did, the *Cutty Sark* cooperated and clawed her way northward. Just as her high, squared stern had kept her from being pooped by the following seas, now her sharp bow kept her slicing cleanly through the waters into the adverse winds. She successfully ran northeast up the Atlantic, crossed the Equator and made her way to the coast of North Africa, then headed north past Portugal. By December 22 she had reached the Bay of Biscay. She was a record-smashing 67 days out of Sydney, and had every reason to expect that she would reach the English Channel in one more day.

Now, so close to home and the finish line, came an agonizing series of delays. First the wind came blowing southwest down the Channel. Beating into it, the *Cutty Sark* was able to move only a miserable 64 miles on December 23, only 65 the next day. On December 25 she made a meager 70 miles, and the crew was dull-spirited in its celebration of Christmas.

The day after that the wind dropped; and on the 27th came a flat calm, a rarity in winter on the blustery English Channel. The hours dragged on and the *Cutty Sark* seemed hardly to move at all.

Not until late in the day did a breeze stir out of the southwest, picking up strength as it came on. Soon a ripple formed at the *Cutty Sark's* bow, growing into a wave. Now the *Cutty Sark* put her shoulder down and surged ahead. At 11 o'clock on the morning of December 28 Woodget and the crew made out Beachy Head, at the southern tip of England, and by 1:25 p.m. they were able to take a pilot aboard for the last leg of the journey. But later in the afternoon a snowstorm swept down the Channel from the north-northwest, reducing visibility to nil, and it was 11:30 p.m. before the *Cutty Sark* finally anchored in the Downs.

Woodget and his men—having spent five days covering only 305 miles—had half expected to hear from the pilot that the *Thermopylae* had long since tied up to her wharf. To their great joy, she had done no

*In a vast, multitiered warehouse known as the great wool floor, workers weigh some of the 700,000 bales of wool that reached London by clipper every year during the 1880s. Some days as many as 3,000 bales entered the warehouse, and so much loose wool drifted about, said The Illustrated London News, that people "frequently walk knee-deep" in it.*

such thing. Not for another week did she come in, logging 80 days. The rest of the wool fleet of 1885 straggled in over the next three weeks. The *Cutty Sark*, 73 days from Sydney, was the undisputed winner of the wool race of 1885.

December 29 dawned clear and cold in London—so cold that, after the crew had washed down the deck of their proud vessel, they had to sweep away sheets of ice. But nothing could chill the warmth of the jubilation that all of them felt. Old White Hat lost no time in coming to share their triumph.

Seven weeks later, when the *Cutty Sark* made ready to sail on her next voyage, he came aboard again, this time with a party of friends and a large brown paper package. He led the visitors on a tour of the ship, then served sandwiches and wine in the main saloon, passing out cigars and raising a toast to Captain Woodget. Afterward, he led the party to the quarter-deck, carrying with him the brown paper parcel. When he opened it, out came a surprise for all—and a present for the ship herself. It was a gilded weather vane, about three feet tall, cut in the form of the witch's cutty sark.

Willis commanded the senior apprentice to put the weather vane in place. Up the rigging the boy scrambled, and as he did so Old White Hat's voice rang out across the Thames, expressing the shared excitement of all those present. Echoing Tam o'Shanter's praise for the beautiful witch, he bellowed: "Weel done, *Cutty Sark.*"

For Woodget and for the *Cutty Sark*, the nine years that followed their first feat together were the best years of their lives. He drove her on nine more voyages between London and Sydney, and she willingly complied, never taking as much as 100 days (the normal length of passage before his time), and only twice exceeding 90 days. And every year she beat the onetime champion *Thermopylae*.

Not only could she beat her own kind, she could on occasion beat the newfangled steamers that were displacing sail from the seas. On July 25, 1889, the new mail steamer *Britannia* came up astern of the *Cutty Sark* off the coast of Australia. The winds were light, and the *Britannia* steamed past. Watching her from his deck, Woodget remarked to one of his officers, "If the wind would freshen up a bit, we would give those passengers something to look at." A bit later the winds did pick up, and Woodget was prepared, with all sails flying. During the night the officer of the deck aboard the *Britannia* spotted riding lights he could not identify. He so noted in the log, and then woke the captain to report that a sailing ship was passing the *Britannia* at a speed he reckoned to be about 17 knots. The next morning, as the steamer entered Sydney Harbor, her crew and passengers found to their astonishment that the *Cutty Sark* was already at anchor; the men on the yardarm were wrapping the final gaskets around her mainsail. The crew and the passengers of the *Britannia* joined in cheering the *Cutty Sark* as the steamer slipped past her.

Woodget himself enjoyed these years to the fullest. He ran his ship his own way, even on occasion defying Jock Willis. Willis liked to have all his ships' boats painted black on their topsides and white underneath.

*The gift of a doting owner, this sheet-metal representation of a cutty sark, or short chemise, was installed as a weather vane on the Cutty Sark after a record-breaking run from Sydney in 1885. The emblem vanished 31 years later and remained lost until 1960, when it turned up for auction in London and was bought by the Cutty Sark Society.*

Inspecting the *Cutty Sark* one day, Willis immediately noticed that her boats were painted all white. He confronted Woodget and demanded to know why. "Because they look better white," Woodget snapped. Old Jock understood the virtues of indulging a good commander; the boats remained white.

Not surprisingly, Woodget had hobbies as unorthodox as some of his orders; the only wonder is that so hard-driving a captain found time to indulge them aboard ship. He kept a bicycle in his cabin and rode it about the 'tween deck—an open area between the main deck and the cargo hold that also sometimes served him as a roller-skating rink.

Owing to the dilatory loading procedures in the Australian wool trade, Woodget and his crew were familiar faces in Sydney. Customarily the clippers arrived during the months of June, July and August to take advantage of the best weather for the outbound passage; however, the sheep in the stations of the Outback would not be sheared until September and October.

For the crewmen and the apprentices, the time in Australia represented an idyllic respite from the rigors of manning a clipper at sea. They always had shore leave to enjoy the pubs and the hospitable girls of boomtown Sydney. There were picnics on Australia's spectacular beaches, sailboat regattas in Sydney's huge harbor and much fraternizing among the clippers.

One well-loved pastime was communal singing. On a still evening with the clippers gathered at their anchorage, the men of one ship would start a chantey. Soon it would be taken up on another ship, then another and another. Presently the harbor echoed with the harmonies of a dozen crews. Occasionally one crew would sing a verse, the entire fleet joining in the chorus, another crew taking the next verse, and the chantey thus proceeding through the fleet. Many of the sailors played harmonicas, fiddles and other musical instruments, and the symphony could be heard downwind for several miles.

Such idleness, while great sport for the seamen and the young apprentices, became increasingly costly for the owners. By 1895 larger sailing ships built of steel—the windjammers—were proving sturdier and more economical than the dainty clipper ships; they could carry six times the tonnage with fewer than twice as many crewmen. Even more threatening were the steamers. With improved reciprocating engines, steamers became safer and more dependable. They could be relied on to maintain speed over a long distance and in all kinds of weather. The *Cutty Sark* might romp past the *Britannia* in a strong breeze, but in the long run of an ocean voyage the steamer was an almost certain winner. Nor were fueling problems the restraint they once had been: The estab-

*In a dramatic vindication of those who still preferred sail to steam power, the Cutty Sark overtakes the mail steamer Britannia—then reputed to be the world's fastest ship—off the Australian coast in July 1889. Sailing at a brisk 17 knots, the Cutty Sark passed her rival during the night—rather than in daylight, as shown in this painting—and dropped anchor at Sydney the next morning a half hour before the steamer.*

lishment of new coaling stations enabled steamships to reach almost anywhere in the world. Toward the middle of the 1890s steamers were encroaching on the wool trade, just as they had on the tea trade a decade and a half before.

Not surprisingly, then, when Woodget returned to London in 1895 after a decade of sailing with the *Cutty Sark*, he found that Old White Hat was selling her. Willis might still love the vessel, but he was a businessman, and after 26 years she had served his purposes. A Portuguese firm bought her for the bargain price of £2,100—scarcely 12 per cent of the sum for which Willis had contracted to have her built. Shortly thereafter, Woodget retired from the sea. He bought a farm in his native Norfolk, where he raised pigs, rabbits, chickens, ducks and geese, and lived to the ripe old age of 82.

Together with the *Thermopylae*, the *Cutty Sark* survived as a working vessel into the 20th Century. The *Thermopylae* was bought in the same year, 1895, by the Portuguese Navy; she was renamed the *Pedro Nunes* and used as a training ship. In 1907, after nearly 40 years of service—more than twice the life span of the usual clipper ship—she was finally judged to have had her day. She was towed to sea and given an honorable burial—sunk in the Atlantic with all her flags flying.

The *Cutty Sark*, meanwhile, went right on sailing. Her new Portuguese owners officially gave her their family name, calling her the *Ferreira*. But so firmly established was her name and her character that the Portuguese crews continued to refer to her affectionately as the *Pequena Camisola*—a literal translation into Portuguese of the *Little Chemise*.

Incredibly, she was still in service as a merchant ship in 1922, at the age of 53. That year she was driven by a Channel storm into Falmouth harbor, where she was spied by British Captain Wilfred Dowman, a retired sailing master who ran a training ship for boys. Although her gold leaf had long since vanished and her bright brass was obscured by crusted paint, the *Cutty Sark* worked her ineffable magic still. Dowman had never forgotten the day when, as an apprentice aboard the clipper *Hawksdale* nearly 30 years before, he had watched the graceful *Cutty Sark* sail smartly past his own ship. He promptly bought her from her Portuguese owners—who asked and got the price of £3,750.

Dowman devoted more than a year to repairing and rerigging her, then used her as a training ship in Cornwall. There, and later at Greenhithe, Kent—after Dowman's widow had given the ship to the Incorporated Thames Nautical Training College—the *Cutty Sark* served to teach British seamen the high art of sail over a period of more than a quarter of a century. In 1952 the *Cutty Sark* Preservation Society was formed under the auspices of the Duke of Edinburgh for the purpose of restoring the ship as nearly as possible to her original self. By 1954 sufficient funds had been raised, and three tugs towed the venerable clipper on her last voyage to a specially built dry dock in Greenwich, where the restoration work began.

From that day forward her tapering mast tips were to dominate the Greenwich waterfront, calling to mind the words of her first captain, George Moodie, who pronounced her "a grand ship, and a ship that will last forever."

*Lying at her permanent berth in Greenwich, England, after a career of more than 50 years, the Cutty Sark evokes the majesty of the clipper breed with her towering masts and 10 miles of rigging. She is the sole survivor of the clipper era.*

# Down-easters: a last echo of a vanishing tradition

A mere decade after the last tumultuous tea races, only a handful of clippers remained at sea, aging relics of a brilliant but brief-blooming era of sail. In their wake, giant steel-hulled windjammers had appeared, and this new breed of behemoths would soon come to dominate the world's long-distance sailing routes.

But in the seaside towns of Maine—downwind and east of the old shipyards of New York and Boston—a proud and crusty band of shipbuilders continued to construct wooden vessels in the clipper tradition. These ships, called "down-easters" for their Maine origins, constituted the last generation of wooden square-riggers.

Though descended from the clippers in hull design and rig, the down-easters were not so fine-lined or loftily sparred as their glamorous American and English forebears. In consequence, the hefty Maine square-riggers were somewhat slower. But their moderately proportioned rigs also meant that the down-easters required only a fraction of a clipper's crew, making it far easier to turn a profit on each voyage. And, whereas the speedy clippers of the 1850s and 1860s depended on premium cargoes of fresh-picked tea and express freight, the down-easters carried bulk goods such as wheat, coal and sugar, whose quality and value were not jeopardized by a small sacrifice in time of delivery.

From the 1860s through the early 1890s, Maine's shipbuilders launched hundreds of sturdy down-easters. The largest was the mighty *Roanoke (right)*, built by Samuel Sewall of Bath, Maine, in 1892. With a cargo capacity of 5,400 tons, the *Roanoke* was bigger than any other wooden vessel afloat. Some 1,250,000 board feet of pine and 25,000 cubic feet of oak were used in the construction of her massive 350-foot hull—more than twice as long as the hulls of early China clippers.

Despite her Gargantuan dimensions, the *Roanoke* proved to be a good sailer that could be handled by a crew of only 30 men, including officers. She made 10 profitable voyages to such distant ports as Shanghai and Manila before a fire destroyed her while she was at anchor in New Caledonia in 1905. By then, even Maine's most stubborn holdouts had surrendered to the fashion for steel: The *Roanoke* was the last wooden square-rigger Sam Sewall ever built—a fitting farewell to a glorious tradition.

*With two steam tugs securing the giant vessel to keep her from smashing into the opposite bank of the Kennebec River on launching, the newly completed Roanoke slips down her ways on August 22, 1892. But, according to an account in the Bath Daily Times, "the ship went so fast that the hawser on the bow of the tugs was snapped in two like tape line." The Roanoke's crew hastily dropped anchor and brought the vessel to a halt.*

At a New York wharf, stevedores load the Roanoke with goods and provisions for a voyage to Australia in 1904. The wheellike device above the ship's rail is a windmill with its miniature sails furled; at sea it served to power a bilge pump.

Readying the Roanoke for departure, a shore gang of professional ship riggers starts hoisting a square sail by hand (above), then uses the ship's large capstan (right) to winch the heavy canvas up to its yard. Altogether, the Roanoke carried 15,000 square yards of canvas on four masts, including a 95-foot-wide mainsail that weighed half a ton when dry—and about twice as much when wet.

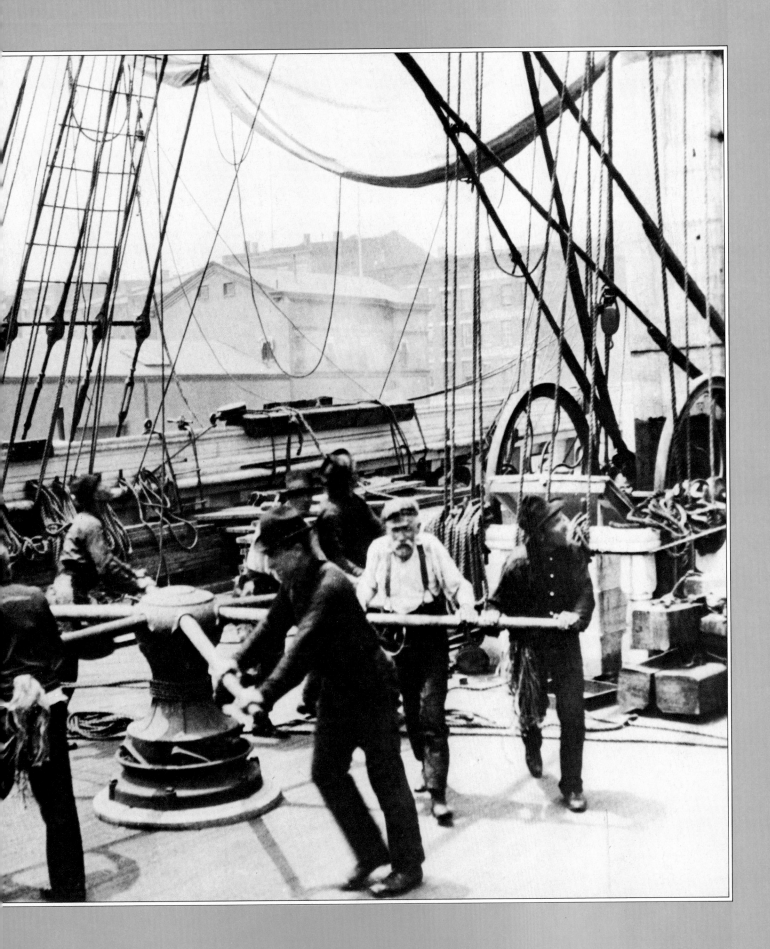

With a full suit of sails, the Roanoke stands out to sea in a gentle breeze. The full-bodied vessel was slow and difficult to handle in light winds, but fast in heavy weather. In 1898 she made a 102-day passage from San Francisco to New York—about three weeks off the best clipper runs but twice as fast as an average voyage in preclipper days.

# Bibliography

Albion, Robert Greenhalgh, *The Rise of New York Port*. Charles Scribner's Sons, 1967.

Brettle, Robert E., *The Cutty Sark: Her Designer and Builder: Hercules Linton, 1836-1900*. Cambridge, England: W. Heffer & Sons, 1969.

Carr, Frank G. G.:

"The Restoration of the *Cutty Sark*." Royal Institute of Naval Architects, London, 1965.

"The Story of the *Cutty Sark*." National Maritime Museum, London, 1966.

Chapelle, Howard I., *The Search for Speed under Sail*. Bonanza Books, 1967.

Chase, Mary Ellen, *Donald McKay and the Clipper Ships*. Houghton Mifflin, 1959.

Cutler, Carl C., *Greyhounds of the Sea: The Story of the American Clipper Ship*. G. P. Putnam's Sons, 1930.

Daniel, Hawthorne, *The Clipper Ship*. Dodd, Mead, 1928.

Dillon, Richard H., *Bully Waterman*. Roxburghe Club, 1956.

Fairburn, William, *Merchant Sail*. Vols. 1-6. Fairburn Marine Education Foundation, 1945-1955.

Florent, Jerry G., ed., *With All Possible Sails Set: The Story of America's Fastest Clipper Ship, the Flying Cloud*. Hallmark Cards, 1979.

Howe, Octavius T., and Frederick C. Matthews, *American Clipper Ships, 1833-1858*. Argosy Antiquarian, 1967.

Klamkin, Marian, *Marine Antiques*. Dodd, Mead, 1975.

LaGrange, Helen, *Clipper Ships of America and Great Britain, 1833-1869*. G. P. Putnam's Sons, 1936.

Laing, Alexander, *The Clipper Ships and Their Makers*. G. P. Putnam's Sons, 1966.

Lubbock, Basil:

*The China Clippers*. Glasgow: Brown, Son & Ferguson, 1946.

*The Log of the "Cutty Sark."* Glasgow: Brown, Son & Ferguson, 1924.

Lyon, Jane D., *Clipper Ships and Captains*. American Heritage, 1962.

MacGregor, David R.:

*Clipper Ships*. Watford, England: Argus Books, 1979.

*Fast Sailing Ships: Their Design and Construction, 1775-1875*. Heassner Publishing, 1973.

*The Tea Clippers*. London: Percival Marshall, 1952.

McKay, Richard C., *Some Famous Sailing Ships and Their Builder, Donald McKay*. G. P. Putnam's Sons, 1928.

Maury, Matthew Fontaine:

*Explanations and Sailing Directions to Accompany the Wind and Current Charts*. 6th ed. E. C. and J. Biddle, 1854. *The Physical Geography of the Sea*. 2nd ed. Harper & Brothers, 1857.

Samuels, Samuel, *From the Forecastle to the Cabin*. Harper & Brothers, 1887.

Stammers, Michael, *The Passage Makers*. Brighton: Teredo Books, 1978.

Summersell, Charles G., *The Journal of George Townley Fullam*. University of Alabama Press, 1973.

Train, George Francis, *My Life in Many States and in Foreign Lands*. D. Appleton, 1902.

Villiers, Alan, *The Cutty Sark: Last of a Glorious Era*. London: Hodder and Stoughton, 1953.

Wayland, John W., *The Pathfinder of the Seas*. Garrett & Massie, 1930.

# Acknowledgments

The index for this book was prepared by Gale Partoyan. The editors wish to thank the following: Roy H. Andersen, artist, and William A. Baker, consultant *(pages 72-79)*; John Batchelor, artist, and David R. MacGregor, consultant *(pages 140-143)*; Bill Hezlep, artist *(page 109)*; Peter McGinn, artist *(endpaper maps)*; Herbert Scott, artist, and William A. Baker, consultant *(page 56)*.

The editors also wish to thank: In Australia: Sydney—C. L. Hume, Maritime Historian. In the United Kingdom: London—Vice Admiral Sir Patrick Bayly, Captain A. V. Bruce, *Cutty Sark* Society; S. W. Wade, Frost and Reed; Lynn Freall, Malcolm Barr Hamilton, David Lyon, Joan Moore, Denis Stonham, National Maritime Museum; Bertram Newbury, Parker Gallery; Frank G. G. Carr, World Ship Trust Project; Brighton—Alex A. Hurst; Eastbourne—Mabel Brettle; Guildford—Hilda Cheesman; Liverpool—Michael Stammers, Merseyside County Museums; Sussex—Leslie A. Wilcox. In France: Paris—Hervé Cras, Director for Historial Studies, Musée de la Marine.

The editors also wish to thank: In the United States: Washington, D.C.—Russ Sherazee, John Ulrich, Defense Mapping Agency; Sharon Gibbs, Center for Polar and Scientific Archives, National Archives; Nadya Makovenyi, Department of Exhibits, William Earl Geoghagen, Jim Knowles, Department of Transportation, Division of Maritime History, Smithsonian Institution; Barbara Lynch, Navy Department Library, John C. Reilly Jr., Ships History, Naval Historical Center, Washington Navy Yard. Elsewhere in the United States: Bath, Maine—Ralph Linwood Snow, Director, Marnee Small, Assistant Curator, Maine Maritime Museum; Berkeley, California—James Hart, Director, The Bancroft Library, University of California; Bethesda, Maryland—William Blair; Boston, Massachusetts—Carl Crossman, Childs Gallery; William B. Osgood, Vice President, State Street Bank & Trust Company; Cambridge, Massachusetts—Bruce M. Lane; Clearwater, Florida—Kenneth Savage; Kings Point, Long Island, New York—Beverly Seeger, American Merchant Marine Museum, U.S. Merchant Marine Academy; Los Angeles, California—Robert A. Weinstein; Mamaroneck, New York—Rudolph J. Schaefer Sr.; Marblehead, Massachusetts—F. Abbot Goodhue; John Merrow, Director, Marblehead Historical Society; Elmira Potter; Milton, Massachusetts—Dr. H. A. Crosby Forbes, Director, William Sargeant, Museum of the American China Trade; Mystic, Connecticut—Revell Carr, Director, Ben Fuller, Curator, Philip Budlong, Richard Malley, Mystic Seaport Museum; New York, New York—Philip B. Kunhardt Jr., Managing Editor, *Life*; Esther Brumberg, Photo Librarian, Museum of the City of New York; Sue Gillies, The New-York Historical Society; George D. Wintress, Vice President, The Seamen's Bank for Savings; Norman Brouwer, South Street Seaport Museum; Newport News, Virginia—Alexander C. Brown; Larry Duane Gilmore, Assistant Curator, Department of Collections, Paul Hensley, Archivist, Katie Bragg, The Mariners Museum; Salem, Massachusetts—Kathy Flynn, Peabody Museum of Salem; San Francisco, California—Warren R. Howell, John Howell Books; Karl Kortum, Director, Karen A. Kines, L. Wilson, National Maritime Museum at San Francisco; Searsport, Maine—C. Gardner Lane Jr., Director, Penobscot Marine Museum; Seattle, Washington—Evelyn and T. Byron Hunt; Whitehall, Virginia—Susan Bryan.

Valuable sources of quotations were *Greyhounds of the Sea: The Story of the American Clipper Ship* by Carl C. Cutler, G. P. Putnam's Sons, 1930; *Bully Waterman* by Richard H. Dillon, The Roxburghe Club, 1956; and *Some Famous Sailing Ships and Their Builder, Donald McKay* by Richard C. McKay, G. P. Putnam's Sons, 1928.

# Picture Credits

# Index

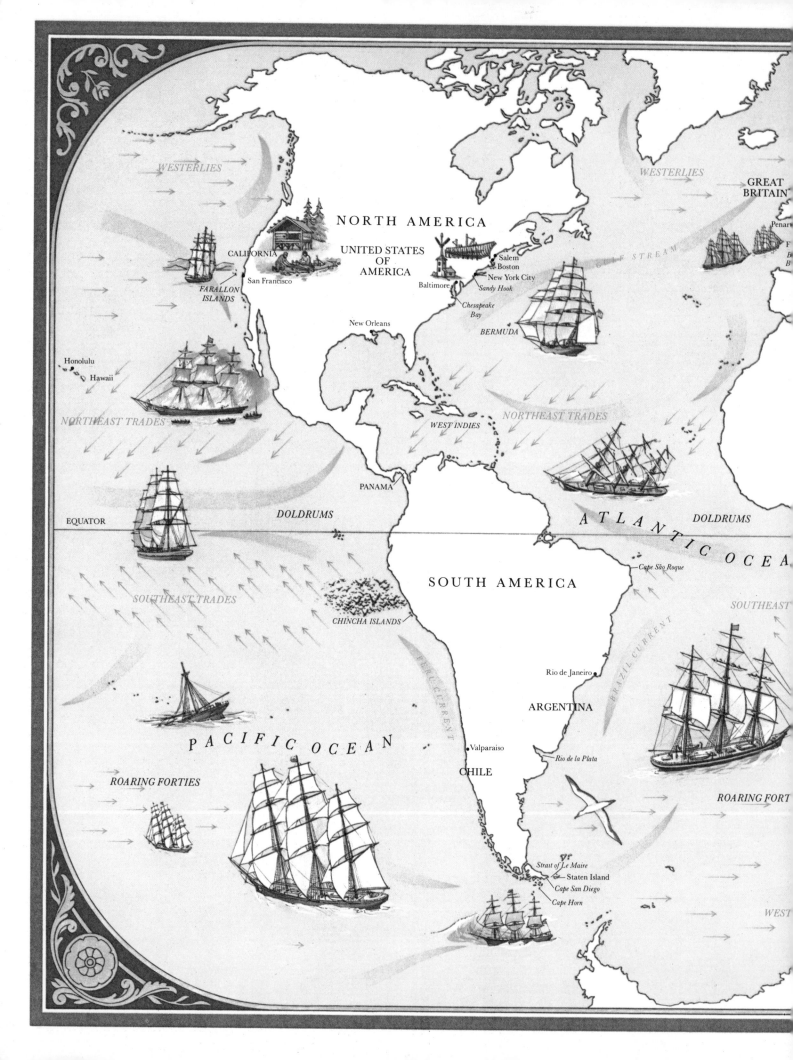